BEING GOOD

*Rethinking Classroom Management
and Student Discipline*

Steven Wolk

HEINEMANN
PORTSMOUTH, NH

Heinemann
A division of Reed Elsevier Inc.
361 Hanover Street
Portsmouth, NH 03801–3912
www.heinemann.com

Offices and agents throughout the world

Cataloging-in-Publication Data is on file at the Library of Congress

ISBN: 0-325-00426-9

Editor: Leigh Peake
Production service: Colophon
Production editor: Sonja S. Chapman
Cover design: Catherine Hawkes, Cat & Mouse Design
Cover and interior photographs: Steven Wolk
Compositor: LeGwin Associates
Manufacturing: Steve Bernier

Printed in the United States of America on acid-free paper

06 05 04 03 02 DA 1 2 3 4 5

For Max,
a good kid

Contents

Acknowledgments

I want to thank the following folks for helping make this book both possible and better: Leigh Peake, Sonja Chapman, and Peg Latham (at Heinemann and Colophon); Laura Gordon and her wonderful fifth-grade class; Amyra Smyrecky and her wonderful class of fourth and fifth graders; my wife, Laura, who helps make everything possible; and my son, Max, who not only reminds me what a good kid is, but teaches me what a good parent should be. Finally, nearing the completion of this book, my Mom, Wilma Joy Wolk, suddenly passed away. Shortly after that the Dean of the College of Education at my university, Nan Giblin, read a portion of the manuscript and told me that she was sure I did not write this book alone. She said, "Your mom helped you write this book." She is exactly right. Thanks, Mom.

Thoughtful Classroom Management

I believe very strongly that the most important
aspects of education are moral and that the term
"moral education" is largely redundant.
                                  —David Purpel (1999)

This book is about what many teachers worry about most: classroom management, behavior, and discipline. My purpose is to look at these issues from a different perspective than they're traditionally considered. There are many assumptions about children's behavior (or misbehavior) in school, and what most consider to be good classroom management and "correct" behavior. This book offers an alternative way for teachers to think about and implement classroom management and deal with issues of student behavior, both bad and good. My hope is that it will encourage teachers to be critical of traditional beliefs about managing a classroom and dealing with student behavior issues, and begin to look at them in different ways.

This book is also about teaching character. In these pages I'm advocating a philosophy (and specific teaching ideas) for character education, which is gaining in popularity because our society and our politicians seem to believe that our children are lacking in morals. I find this ironic because adults cause the vast majority of the misery in the world. If there were some kind of national troublemaking index, I have no doubt that adults would rate far higher than kids. Adults start all wars, commit the vast majority of violence, lie to their bosses and friends and spouses, cheat on their taxes, break the speed limit, create and market horrendously violent video games, and eat grapes in grocery store produce departments. It is adults who have mastered corruption and manipulation in our corporations, governments, and media. Yet, oddly, adults point fingers at our children as if kids are the ones in need of strict discipline, moral help, and character education.

Still, I happen to agree that teachers should be teaching for character. Unfortunately, the way that's usually done in schools is with character education "programs," which are usually as scripted as textbooks and worksheets. Teaching character this way is an oxymoron. Packaged character education programs are created for the masses, whereas they really need to be created for and *evolve from* each unique classroom. And classroom management and issues of character are both essentially about goodness and how we act, in school and out. So for me, classroom management and character education are synonymous or at least woven together like a double helix strand of DNA. If teachers implement their classroom management from a thoughtful and democratic perspective similar to the ideas in this book, they already are educating for character. I also believe there is no separation between the content we teach (math, social studies, art, science, etc.) and issues of character and morality. They are just as intertwined. The knowledge of that content should inform and direct the daily moral decisions we make.

All of these issues—classroom management, behavior, character, subject matter knowledge, and morality—should all be intertwined with both *citizenship* and *social justice*. As teachers we are not just creating educated people; we are helping to create citizens of a democracy. This means nurturing in children the habits of mind to participate actively in our daily democracy; live and act for the common good; and work to create a better, more humane, just, and equal society and world. Being an informed citizen, practicing critical literacy, making decisions at least in part based on some kind of a personal moral code, and being active—and perhaps even activist—in creating a more just world are about good character and good citizenship; they are one and the same. And by encouraging our students to live a life free of racism, prejudice, sexism, and homophobia; to appreciate cultural diversity; and to help end economic, cultural, and gender inequality, we are teaching a curriculum for social justice. So all of these ideas—student behavior, classroom management, character, citizenship, social justice, and the "academic" content—should be seen as an intertwined and symbiotic "whole" of our teaching. For Sheldon Berman (1997) this would be teaching children *social responsibility*. He writes:

> Teaching social responsibility incorporates the development of social skills, ethics, and character. Although it also includes developing political knowledge and skills, it gives primary attention to the way we live with others and our responsibility for furthering the common good. Therefore, unlike citizenship education, social responsibility cuts across the curriculum and the culture and organization of the school. It adds to the commonly accepted notions of citizenship education the concepts that young people must be able to work with and care for others, that classrooms and schools need to embody and nurture a sense of responsibility through their organization and governance, and that these themes can be integrated into all areas of the curriculum. (p. 14)

Being Good as a Journey

Classroom management typically includes the following: how teachers structure their classrooms; their implicit and explicit rules and expectations; their philosophies of teaching, learning, and human nature; and how teachers deal with issues of student behavior and discipline. I must say that I don't like the phrase *classroom management*. It sounds as if I were a *manager of workers* rather than a *teacher of human beings*. A classroom must have a sense of order, some underlying structure. But order and structure do not have to mean kids being quiet and sitting still—and me, the teacher, managing that orderliness—as in the traditional paradigm of classroom management. In contrast to that, the order and structure of a classroom can mean kids and teachers living and working in a caring classroom space doing purposeful, meaningful, and thoughtful learning—with the order and structure and character education as an inherent part of everything that happens in that space. Do kids need to "be good" to make that happen? Yes they do. But kids sitting silently and staying "on task" is not necessarily "being good," especially if that behavior is externally controlled.

Goodness is in our hearts and minds. True goodness comes from *within*, and that's the goal of a more democratic philosophy of classroom management: helping kids become managers of themselves by helping them to develop and shape their "self," including character and self-discipline. That's where the title of this book comes from. "Being good" does not simply mean kids have good behavior, but rather, that they are thinking and learning about their behavior and how it affects others. To me, being good is not so much about kids reaching a final "good behavior" destination, but rather helping them to make the never-ending journey. Given this, the best "goodness" a person (or student) can have is consciously *striving* and *learning* to be good, and grappling with what that means in all of its complexity.

Getting kids to take this journey is not easy and it does not happen quickly. It is a slow process. Deep change, even in young children, usually takes time. But it is still certainly worthwhile. There is a profound difference between a student walking into a classroom and being good because that's what school or the teacher demands, and a student walking into a classroom and being good as a true part of his or her being. Most of these changes in students are small, so you rarely see sweeping transformations. One day you may hear a student say "thank you"; or you may see a student choosing to focus on creating a group play when someone else in the group is choosing to fool around; or a student may suddenly write an empathetic comment in his or her journal. These kinds of behaviors are fleeting and they may appear "small," but day after day, week after, month after month, they add up. The real power is cumulative.

And these changes can be so subtle that the kids themselves don't even see them. I had a third-grade student a few years ago I'll call Angie. For the entire year Angie was very immature. She argued with other kids (and me). She got mad and rarely recognized the world filled with people beyond her world. Angie was in my class for fourth grade, too, and during the beginning of that year I started seeing amazing changes in her. She was becoming respectful and thoughtful of other people. She soon became the most helpful student in the class, not only to me, but also to the other kids. I went out of my way to tell Angie what I was seeing, to compliment her, to thank her, to help her build success from success. Two things were clear to me about Angie: She was very proud of her growth and she was surprised herself. This is not to say that I was the one person who made that happen. Her parents certainly played a huge role, maybe her friends helped, and being a year older helped. But I also believe that what we were doing in our classroom played a role as well in her wonderful changes. Did I see these kinds of great character changes often? Not really. Again, most were smaller. But seeds were planted and characters were shaped.

This is not a book of answers. This is a book of ideas. When I taught elementary school I had my share of behavior problems and I struggled with many of them, just like other teachers. Many of them I did not "solve" either. I make no claim that any of the ideas in this book will "work" for any particular student or class or school. But take the ideas you like and try them out, discard the rest, or save them for a rainy day to mull over. I encourage you to change them, cut them up, make them your own, shape them to fit you and your students, use them as a place to start. Ideas are like snowballs; let's all keep rolling them around, trying them out, giving them shape and substance, making them better.

Seeing the Whole of Classroom Management

Educators generally talk about classroom management and student behavior as if they exist in a vacuum, not connected to other happenings in the classroom, the school, or society. Because of this, far too often teachers attempt to deal with classroom management issues in isolation from the rest of their work and their students' learning. To honestly address these issues we must see them systemically, as a connected part of everything else that is happening in the classroom. The behavior of kids in school is not only about their behavior. There is a lot going on within the walls of their classrooms—as well as within society itself—that influences that behavior, so we must examine the larger contexts carefully and critically. We must see the "whole" of classroom management and understand its complexity.

First is the teaching. Teachers teach so kids can learn. (That's the general idea, anyway.) Traditionally, the classroom management is done so the teachers can teach and the kids can (supposedly) learn. But the way teachers manage their classrooms cannot be viewed as if that managing is something *separate* from the teaching and the learning. In school, the teaching of kids and their learning (or lack of learning) is intricately connected to how we manage them. How we manage our classrooms *is* our teaching as much as a reading curriculum is our teaching.

Many educators have commented that our schools are unfortunately based on a paradigm of control (Kohn, 1993; McNeil, 1988; Smith, 1986). Traditional teaching methods, such as kids remaining at their desks, teacher lecture with silent students, rigidly predetermined curriculums, worksheets and textbooks, and testing are used because they perform the dual role of teaching content and controlling students. But just because a classroom is quiet and orderly doesn't mean anyone is learning anything. One of the myths of teaching is the assumption that children are learning (or should be learning) *because* they're quiet and orderly. It's easy to assume that a classroom of well-behaved students has a lot of learning going on, but just because kids are well-behaved doesn't automatically mean they're learning anything; it means they're under control and doing what they are told to do. Consider a study done by Mihaly Csikszentmihalyi (1993). He gave entire high school classes and their teachers beepers and "beeped" them simultaneously. They filled out a sheet right as they were beeped, and answered questions such as, "What are you doing right now?" and "What are you thinking about right now?" Csikszentmihalyi describes a typical response:

> In a typical history classroom where a teacher is lecturing about Genghis Kahn's invasion of China and conquest of Beijing in 1215, only 2 out of 27 students were thinking about China when they were signaled. One of the 2 was remembering the meal he had when he last ate out with his family at a Chinese restaurant, and the other student was wondering why Chinese men wore their hair in a ponytail. None mentioned Genghis Khan, Beijing, or 1215. (p. 196, n2)

As teachers we cannot assume that even well-behaved and "on task" students are meaningfully learning or even thinking about what is being taught. Making the control of students and orderly and efficient classrooms a first priority of school results in the *illusion of learning*. Lots of kids are quiet most of the time, doing their homework, taking tests, writing essays, reading textbooks, getting decent grades. But are they consciously and intellectually engaged and meaningfully learning, or is most of that "content" put into short-term memory for the test or the essay and then forgotten? The traditional paradigm (or method) of teaching is done more for its mechanisms of controlling children than for its efficacy of meaningful learning. This belief system of teaching is so entrenched in our culture that society now equates the two and assumes that children *can't* learn *unless* they're silently sitting at a desk listening to a teacher. This stands in deep contrast to the fact that the vast majority of my learning—perhaps 99 percent of everything I know—I did not learn in the orderly classrooms of my childhood but in the messy, noisy, and largely spontaneous reality of my daily life.

Rather than teaching in ways that are based on control, we need classrooms that are purposeful, thoughtful, and creative. In purposeful classrooms kids are working toward individual and collective goals because the work they are doing is interesting and intellectual and makes connections to the children's lives. Classrooms that are purposeful have order, but it is an order that comes from the "moving spirit" (Kilpatrick, 1918) of the classroom community, from the relevant and purposeful activities in which the kids are engaged, and hopefully from the self-discipline of the students. On its surface this book is about classroom management, but in reality it is about everything teachers do in their classrooms, and especially our teaching, because how we teach directly influences how our students act.

Behavior and Character as Curriculum

The purpose of school should be much more than just teaching kids the "facts" and skills of reading, writing, math, science, and social studies. Just like us adults, children are complex human beings who bring all of themselves into the classroom: cognitive, affective, moral, political, spiritual. As educators it is our responsibility to recognize, celebrate, and help shape all of these facets of our students. All of these different "ways of knowing" are woven together like a fine blanket creating our whole self, so if we ignore one of them we limit the entire person. Patrick Shannon (1995) has written that teachers are in the "identity creation" business. To do that, to help children consciously shape their identities means consciously going beyond the official curriculum—which is overwhelmingly dominated by "facts" and skills—and making behavior, community, character, citizenship, and social justice a part of the classroom curriculum.

Curriculum is traditionally viewed simplistically. Most people assume that curriculum is strictly the academic content of a school or a classroom. Typically, curriculum includes textbooks, worksheets, spelling lists, a movie a teacher shows on the Great Depression, tests given, a novel a class reads, an assigned essay, and so on. But this is a very narrow way to define curriculum. In contrast to that is the idea that curriculum is everything that happens to children in school. As deMarrias and LeCompte (1999) write about curriculum,

> More than the formal content of lessons taught—which is what most people normally think of when they envision curriculum—it is also the method of presentation, the way in which students are grouped in classes, the manner in which time and tasks are organized, and the interaction within classrooms. The term *curriculum* refers to the total school experience provided to students, whether planned or unplanned by educators. (p. 223)

Viewed in this way, curriculum includes everything teachers do, including their classroom management and how they handle student behavior. How teachers manage children and deal with discipline *are* curriculum, just as much as a spelling list, the facts of photosynthesis, and the multiplication table are curriculum.

Teaching Self-Discipline

Too often classroom management is based on a belief system of external control. There are times when explicit direction is needed in a classroom, but as an everyday classroom philosophy it does little to help kids develop self-control and responsibility, or to help them see themselves as members of a larger community. To do this, we must practice classroom management as an *internal* paradigm, meaning we must strive to help our students see themselves as members of larger communities and to grapple with the complex issues of control, freedom, responsibility, and behavior. Doing so can help them to learn to live both in school and out with respectful and productive self-discipline. As well-known pediatrician T. Berry Brazelton (1992) writes, "*Discipline* means 'teaching,' not punishment" (p. 253).

Many people scoff at this notion of self-discipline for kids in school. A kid's job in school, many like to say, is to come in, sit down, be quiet, listen, do the work, and learn. But isn't self-control and thoughtful decision making what good parents help their children learn from the day they're born? Parents do not want to incessantly tell their children what they can and cannot do; they want to help them develop the capacities and responsibilities to make those judgments for themselves. Some people call that maturity. People are mature when they can make good decisions and act respectfully and responsibly. There is an old saying about learning and self-reliance: "Give a person a fish and you feed them for a day; teach a person how to fish and you feed them for a lifetime." The same could be said about behavior: "Control a person's behavior externally and they are responsible for the moment; help a person develop self-discipline and they are responsible for a lifetime."

Some would say that many schools and teachers already teach self-discipline with their various character education programs. This may be true. But again, what I'm writing about here cannot work as a prepackaged program, delivered en masse. Prepackaged programs are usually implemented during a specific time of the school day like a science program or a drama program. Character education programs that do that are telling kids, "Here's our twenty minutes of the day that we think about issues of character." In contrast, character education should permeate the entire classroom experience. No separate "character education" time needs to be scheduled, because helping kids reflect and shape their character is an interwoven part of the everyday curriculum and classroom environment.

Behavior and Democracy

As I wrote previously, classroom management and children's classroom behavior are intimately connected to democracy. Democracy at its best involves people living together in familial, local, national, and global communities. John Dewey wrote, "Democracy is more than a form of government, it is primarily a mode of associated living, of conjoint communicated experiences" (1944/1966, p. 87). Dewey believed the most important kind of democracy was a *way of life*. A democratic way of life was filled with asking questions; engaging in discourse and talk on important issues; keeping informed; having civic courage, being thoughtful, educating and improving the self; and being an active participant in community rather than merely an observer. At their core, these qualities involve how we choose to behave and spend our time. By helping our students explore issues of our in-school and out-of-school behavior, we are teaching and learning about much more than just behavior; we are shaping our entire beings and helping kids create who they want to be and how they want to live as members of those democratic communities. At its best the classroom becomes life itself. We no longer teach about democracy and community, but *live* democracy and community. Susan Adler (2000), past president of the National Council for the Social Studies, refers to classrooms as *public spaces*.

At the heart of this communal democracy is the interaction among people, freedom, our "inalienable" rights, and our civic and moral responsibilities. Perhaps the central issue of a democracy is the behavior of its people. This means we must ask questions of our citizens and our students that go far beyond whether they know when to be quiet and if they follow the rules. We should be asking: Do they think? Are they good community members? Do they participate in civic life? Do they treat others with respect and equality? Do they care about people, living things, and the earth? Do they vote? Do they remain informed of world and local events? Do they make informed decisions? Do they appreciate diversity? Do they obey the laws? Do they question unjust laws and policies? Do they engage in discourse with others about important issues? Are they critical, looking for multiple perspectives on issues and events and history? Are they kind to their neighbors? Do they share their riches? All of these questions have to do with how each of us lives each day, which results in the society and world that is the product of our collective actions. Given that our behavior is so integral to our lives and our democracy—and is an equally important issue in our classrooms—wouldn't it be common sense to use our classrooms to explore these very issues with kids? If we did, maybe we would not only have more thoughtful and peaceful classrooms, but also have a better world.

Time

Understandably, many teachers say that they don't have time to teach kids about self-discipline and behavior because they are overburdened with their existing curricular requirements. I agree, teachers are expected to do a lot, and it is infinitely easier to just control kids externally than to help them learn about self-discipline and thoughtfulness. There is no question that the content "coverage" is enormous. Most teachers have mounds of textbooks to complete by June and are under a lot of pressure to have their students do well on standardized tests.

But even with the tremendous time constraints imposed on teachers, I believe there is a great deal teachers can do. First, no two teachers implement the same curriculum in the same way. All teachers make changes to the official curriculum they're given to teach; they cut some of this out, they speed through that, they add extra time for this, they add something new on their own. In my first teaching job, sixth grade, there were five classrooms all in the same hallway, all using the same official sixth-grade curriculum. But what was actually taught (and learned) in those five classrooms was different, because all five of the teachers taught their own version of the same curriculum, creating, in essence, five different curriculums (Wolk, 1998). If the reality of schooling is that teachers make changes in official curriculums, then they can also make changes in regard to teaching about self-discipline and character. If teachers really want to, most can find some time to do this. But they will rarely be invited to do it, so teachers need to take the initiative.

Second, teachers have made some significant gains in power in the last twenty years. More and more teachers are implementing progressive and experimental pedagogy on their own. Examples of this abound: whole language, integrative curriculum, democratic classrooms, teaching for social justice, constructivist classrooms, "hands-on" math and science, multicultural curriculums, project-based and inquiry-oriented classrooms, authentic and portfolio assessment—even entire public schools are being created and run by teachers (for example, charter schools and the Small Schools Movement.) Historically, teachers have been in a subservient role, but this is slowly beginning to change. The new kind of teacher is highly reflective, respected for knowledge of teaching and learning, looked upon as a professional, a lifelong learner, and may even see oneself as an educational change agent or activist. With this comes more freedom to implement and experiment with innovative ideas. I also believe that most principals would welcome their teachers' devoting time in the school day to help their kids develop self-discipline.

Finally, if a teacher is dealing with poor behavior in the classroom regularly, what good is forging ahead with the required curriculum if the disruptions hinder learning? When I started to teach in a Chicago public school (having moved from a suburban school) I was confronted with behavior problems I never imagined. (I'll have more to say on chronic and serious behavior problems later in the chapter.) Some of my students were constantly disrupting our classroom. I realized that I had to take some serious time away from the required curriculum and work with my students on how (and why) to be good. The alternative was to continue to be frustrated (and have my many well-behaved students frustrated) and, in the end, have little meaningful learning going on. I had to make a decision, and my decision was to focus on the long term: to help my students grow as complete human beings, not just as students of reading or math or social studies.

So, yes, time can be tough, but the problem is not insurmountable. Move things around, don't teach something everyday, eliminate something, combine things, cut something short. Make some time, even if it's twenty minutes, and do something useful with it. And remember that teaching kids to be good should be integrated throughout the day and into the existing curriculum, so teachers don't need to find huge blocks of time to make this happen. You can start by taking one topic that you already teach, say Native Americans or the human body, and ask yourself how you can integrate issues of goodness, social justice, and character.

For example, if you're doing a unit on Native Americans, you can teach a more accurate history of the genocide committed against these peoples than what is typically included in social studies textbooks (Loewen, 1994). You can also include Native American life today (there are two million American Indians). Conditions today on most reservations are terrible; Native Americans have the highest rate of unemployment, alcoholism, and poverty. There are many issues of goodness to be explored here: What should we as a nation be doing to improve the lives of Native Americans? What is the relationship between the past oppressions of Native Americans and their lack of economic well-being today? What might we as a nation owe Native Americans today? The same can be done with the human body. Should we use animals to study diseases? Should we have euthanasia? How have technology and industry negatively affected our health and what should we do about it? What are the health effects from the fast food industry? Most of these questions don't have single "correct" answers, but they can be researched, written about, and discussed. By making these issues a part of what we are already teaching—and by connecting them to children's lives and their moral identities—teachers don't need huge amounts of extra time.

Six Ideas to Consider

Here are six points to think about when considering classroom management, teaching, and student behavior.

Make the Work Interesting and the Discipline Will Take Care of Itself

This is a quote from E.B. White, who wrote *Charlotte's Web*. As teachers we can't ask whether our students are simply behaving; we must ask ourselves what we are expecting them to do for all those hours they're in our classrooms. If students are often sitting in desks, listening to a teacher lecture, filling in worksheets and workbooks, reading dull textbooks, doing a lot of rote work with little voice and choice, and only studying the content and knowledge that other people feel is important to learn, how can we blame them if they rebel with poor behavior and little motivation? This idea says that if we want kids to be engaged in their work in school, if we want them to *care*, then we must make what we're having them do interesting, meaningful, creative, and relevant. If kids truly care about what they're doing, they won't think about goofing around or being "off task."

Many of my education students think the way to do this is by making school *fun*. If school is fun, they think, their students will care about their learning and they won't misbehave. But fun puts the wrong emphasis on what we want to happen in our classrooms. I agree with Bill Ayers (1995) who says that fun is distracting. When I think of fun I think of a comedy movie, a ride on a roller coaster, clowns, a good party, playing in the sprinkler with my son. Is that the kind of environment we want for our classrooms? Learning often involves hard work, and hard work isn't always fun. Rather than focusing on making classrooms fun, we should strive to make them interesting, intellectual, collaborative, fascinating, creative, thoughtful, and relevant.

To be honest, I don't agree with E.B. White completely. I don't believe that in many instances the discipline will take care of *itself*. First, while the kids are learning how to work in a classroom that "makes the work interesting" there might be some problems with behavior and management. This is primarily because that kind of classroom is new to most students, and because years of traditional schooling taught them to be passive, waiting to be "taught to." Kornfield and Goodman (1995) call this student passivity "the glaze." We need to reawaken a love of learning and help kids learn how to work in this kind of classroom. Second, even if the discipline does take care of itself, all children can still benefit from exploring issues of character and self-discipline. In the most well behaved classroom there is a tremendous amount of growth that can take place regarding behavior and character. So, while I agree with E.B. White, it's really not that easy. Teachers must work to make it happen.

Human Beings—Including Children—Are More than Happy to Work Hard and Learn

Douglas McGregor (1960) differentiated between his Theory X and Theory Y of management. McGregor wrote, "Behind every managerial decision or action are assumptions about human nature and human behavior" (p. 87). For most people these assumptions are tacit, or part of our subconscious, but they still direct our actions. Good reflective teaching involves becoming conscious of our tacit knowledge and assumptions (Zeichner & Liston, 1987). Theory X, the "traditional view of direction and control," has three assumptions:

1. Most people have a natural dislike of work and will avoid it.
2. Most people need to be forced and threatened with punishment to work hard.
3. Most people prefer to be directed by others, have little motivation, and want little responsibility.

In great contrast his Theory Y states that human beings will happily work hard, especially for something in which they have a personal stake and some control. Here are two of his six Theory Y assumptions:

1. "Work is as natural as play or rest."
2. People will have "self-direction and self-control in the service of objectives to which he is committed." (pp. 47–48)

Traditional schools overwhelmingly favor Theory X. If they had trust in children, their school day would look extremely different, giving them considerable voice and decision making. The Theory X "punishment" McGregor wrote of is obvious: bad grades, bad checkmarks on report cards, failing a class or a grade level, calls or notes home to parents, having to write something as punishment. All of these are external coercions, strongly framing school within the paradigm of behaviorism, which is all about external control. I agree with Alfie Kohn (1996) who argues that behaviorism not only is the wrong paradigm for our classrooms, but also is actually damaging to children.

I also believe that human beings—including kids—are inherently good. I believe the human animal is biologically good and moral. Yes, many people have done evil things. History is strewn with the horrific realities of that. The twentieth century (the "civilized" century) by far must have been the bloodiest, and perhaps the most amoral, century in the 200,000-year history of humankind (more than one hundred million people killed in wars alone). But still, I have faith in human goodness, and this has many implications for me as an elementary and middle school teacher. I began with the belief that my students were good people, they wanted to be good, they cared for others, they were kind, and they were giving. They didn't always show their goodness; many of them didn't even know they had it; and many had their goodness buried beneath lay-ers of pop culture, consumerism, and a me-first American attitude. But it was there waiting to be challenged and put to good use.

Human beings—including kids—want to learn about and understand their world. Learning and making sense of the world are the primary func-tions of the human brain (Caine & Caine, 1991). When I watch and inter-act with my son, Max, who is four years old, I see evidence every day that this is true. Max is constantly learning, constantly striving to make sense of his environments. For example, when he was younger he developed a brief fascination with rocks. We would be walking along a sidewalk and he'd stop to explore rocks and stones. He wanted to look at them, feel them, hold them, taste them, understand them. As Max interacted with rocks he was learning, and I see this kind of "osmotic learning" (Mayher, 1990) hap-pening every day. What if all of school was like a pile of rocks to Max?

Thoughtful and Democratic Classroom Management Takes Time

Children (and adults) are capable of deep personal transformations, but I have no magic formulas to make these ideas work. I struggled through them just like other teachers struggle. Good learning usually takes time, and this is especially true when you're working to change how children think about their behavior and how they see themselves and the world. Teaching kids self-discipline is a slow process, and the successes are usu-ally small, fleeting details you see just by being in the classroom every day. So, the requirements here for teachers are simple to say and hard to do: be patient, stick with it, limit your headaches, always try to enjoy your work, and celebrate the successes, no matter how seemingly small.

Teaching, Schooling, Behavior, Classroom Management, Discipline, and Classroom Rules All Have a Moral Dimension

Teaching is a moral act. That idea scares many people; they want moral-ity to be left out of the classroom. I don't know how that can be done

because how we act as individuals, how we treat others, how we live mo-
ment-by-moment, the decisions we make, the content we choose to teach,
are all moral choices. It is not possible to teach without all of these issues
occurring in any classroom. Morality, after all, is about goodness and our
actions, and they are a central concern to teachers, society, and an endless
stream of political rhetoric. If, as many people allude, the issues of values,
goodness, character, and morality are central to life and democracy, then
it is imperative that teachers take the initiative in raising kids' consciousness to these issues.

In everything they do teachers make moral choices, which explicitly
and tacitly teach children how they should act and what they should
value. David Hansen (1992) has written of what he calls the "shared
morality" of a classroom, which is a common set of values that a classroom—with the lead of the teacher—constantly works toward. These values, such as caring, kindness, and the common good, are not seen as
"rules," such as "no hitting" or "no running in the halls." Rules have the
assumption (in school, at least) that they are not to be debated. Values,
on the other hand, permeate a classroom's ethos, with the teacher figura-
tively saying, "Here are some ideas that I (and others) value in life, let's
talk about them, think about them, debate them, and maybe we can
come to some mutual understanding of how we should live together."
Helping children develop their moral selves is not about dictating what
their moral identity (Glover, 1999) should be, but about exploring those
issues together and trying to have a meeting of the minds and hearts so
we can live in peace, care for one another, learn together, shape our characters, and create a better world.

The Purpose of School Should Not Be Control—but Freedom

Most schools are obsessed with control. Considering that our nation likes
to flaunt its freedoms, this is tremendously ironic. One of the reasons
many of its classrooms have behavior problems is precisely because
schools want to control everything students do. The pursuit of control
dictates nearly everything that happens in a classroom: the use of textbooks and worksheets; strict schedules; separate subjects; lecture and direct instruction; students doing most of their work by themselves;
avoidance of controversial content; minimal student talking; and adher-
ence to a predetermined curriculum. Perhaps the most pervasive form of
control is standardized testing, hence the word *standardized*.

Why are schools so obsessed with controlling children? I believe it is largely a lack of trust. Most adults don't trust kids to think for themselves, make good decisions, be involved their own learning, and be good. A more democratic classroom management begins with trust in children. This doesn't mean that children are allowed to do whatever they want or that they don't need guidance in being good. Freedom in a democratic society requires order, responsibility, and certain limits. The same is true in a democratic classroom. But this can happen while giving children a real voice in the classroom. And a teacher *can* do this and remain the final authority in the classroom. Giving kids some significant freedom in school can be done in intellectual and "rigorous" classrooms that have high academic and behavioral expectations. I do not think it is possible to nurture a love of lifelong learning in children without giving them some real freedom in their learning.

Teaching Is Messy

In the early twentieth century there was an education movement (or belief system) called "scientific curriculum-making." The underlying belief was that teaching is a science and that by creating a scientifically rigid, programmatic curriculum and technocratic "methods," teachers cannot fail in their teaching. Scientific curriculum making was part of the larger education movement of "social efficiency" or the "social behaviorist" (Kliebard, 1987). This movement saw the purpose of school as being to maintain an efficient society, which really meant putting people in predetermined social roles and economic classes to maintain an "orderly" society to feed our economy. Many educators argue that this is the system—social-efficiency-oriented factory-model schooling—that we still have today. Evidence of this is right in the textbooks teachers are given, which have a complete day-by-day, lesson-by-lesson scope and sequence in an effort to "scientize" our teaching and make it "teacher-proof."

In contrast to a scientific belief system for teaching is a paradigm that sees teaching as an art, a political and moral endeavor, as being very messy, unpredictable, and nonlinear. This is the antithesis of a scientific view of teaching and curriculum. No matter how much planning one does, no matter how many rigid objectives and "standards" one writes, no matter how many tests are given, and no matter how controlled kids and classrooms are, teaching will still be messy, largely because life itself is messy and uncertain. Educating people cannot be done as if we are putting together toasters on an assembly line or mixing chemicals in a laboratory. Human endeavors are inherently unpredictable, context specific, and situated in the unique realities and experiences of the participants. This means that a certain degree of "bad" or messy behavior is inevitable, so we need to redefine what is acceptable classroom behavior, becoming tolerant of this messiness.

The Complexity of Behavior

Many teachers talk about students' "bad behavior." What exactly do they mean? What, specifically, are the kids doing that's bad? We need to remember that poor student behavior and problems with classroom management are relative. Lousy behavior to you may not be lousy behavior to the teacher next door. So, let's try to be specific about some bad behavior. Perhaps the largest category is what is commonly referred to as being "off task." This means that students are not doing what they're supposed to be doing. They are not off all tasks, of course, since they're certainly on their own task, but they are off the teacher's task. Most classrooms have explicit and implicit expectations and rules. When students are told do some schoolwork and they don't follow those expectations, they are "off task."

Being off task says what a child *isn't* doing, but we also need to ask what they *are* doing. If a student is off task, does this automatically mean he or she is behaving poorly? I suppose there's a range of being off task, from a kid momentarily chatting with a classmate to a kid out of his or her seat to sharpen a pencil, from a kid doodling to a kid throwing books out the classroom window. Obviously, the last kid is misbehaving, but what about the other kids? If a student chats with a friend about last night's episode of a TV show while working on a research project, is that bad behavior? How much chatting is too much chatting? And when does harmless chatting become *disruptive* chatting? The notion of a kid being "off task" isn't simple; it's not a question of being either off or on task. There's a wide range of being off task that would result in a wide range of possible consequences and teacher actions, depending on the school, the kid, the teacher, the classroom, and the context of the behavior.

Teachers needs to decide for themselves when a student crosses the line from minor off-task behavior to more serious off-task behavior. (And many of these decisions need to be made on the spot.) I've known teachers who would have a serious problem with a student who gets some tissues without permission. When I taught elementary school, I *expected* a certain amount of off-task chatter, which is exactly what adults do every day at their jobs when they stop to talk with a colleague or make a personal phone call or e-mail. As long as this chatter was kept to a minimum and it wasn't disruptive—that is, it didn't interfere with the class doing our work—I didn't mind it. It added life to the classroom and helped create an informal atmosphere. Still, I've had students that were off task incessantly, which *is* unacceptable behavior, meaning that I had to do something about it.

There is also the proverbial "goofing around" bad behavior. This is not simply being off task; when a student is goofing around they've taken their off-task behavior to a more serious level. The issue is no longer that they aren't doing the required task; now their behavior has become *disruptive*, which means their behavior is hindering the learning of other kids and harming the classroom community. Just like with being off task, there are also degrees of goofing around, from the student who blurts out a joke, to kids laughing and being boisterous, to students screaming as they chase each other around the room (which I've had happen to me), and so on.

The more serious forms of bad behavior would include any form of violent and offensive behavior: fighting or hitting, verbal abuse, sexual or racist comments or harassment (any derogatory comment), serious disruptions that go beyond goofing around, as well as less serious poor behavior that's chronic. These behaviors often result in a school consequence (from the principal). (Of course the decision to involve the principal is usually the teacher's.) If the principal does get involved the range of consequences is wide: from a meeting with the principal (with or without parents) to suspension or expulsion (two options of which I have never understood the logic). Exactly what the principal chooses to do can sometimes involve the teacher's input and sometimes not. Again, it depends. The point here is this: Behavior is complex and requires critical reflection from teachers.

Whether to involve parents when a student has poor behavior can be equally complex. There have been times when a student has done something that could have gotten them suspended, but I chose to handle it myself. There are other instances when I decided to call parents when I didn't have to. For me, there are no steadfast rules about when to call or not to call. I have to consider every situation in its context. I don't believe teachers need to be consistent with consequences; they need to be *fair*, which is different. The former says that a student gets a certain consequence after a specific behavior no matter what, while the latter says that all kids and all situations are different, and as the teacher I need to consider as many variables as I can before making a decision.

What constitutes bad behavior also depends on the goals of the teachers and the kind of classroom they create. The student behavior that's tolerated in a highly active, collaborative, project-based classroom (such as a lot of movement and noise) is rarely tolerated in a traditional classroom where the kids spend most of their time at their desks. Once again we can see that the kind of classroom a teacher creates and the teaching methods used are directly related to students' behavior and our overall philosophy of classroom management; our teaching beliefs and methodologies create a set of tacit "rules" that determine what we consider to be acceptable and unacceptable behaviors. So, in creating (or recreating) a philosophy of classroom management teachers must go beyond how they will manage students and decide how they want to teach. And decisions on how they want to teach should be directly based upon their beliefs of how children learn best and what they believe about human nature. (For example, do you believe children naturally need to move and talk? How we answer this question should influence how we teach.)

There is also a huge difference between bad behavior and lack of enthusiasm or motivation. In my first teaching job I rarely had poor behavior. Many new teachers assume that all teachers have bad behavior in their classrooms, but that's not true. There are many teachers that don't have any serious behavior problems, and I was one of them for my first fours years of teaching. I did, however, have to deal with a lack of enthusiasm from many of my students. They didn't care much about school or learning and put forth minimal effort. These were *not* behavior problems, or even a problem with my classroom management, but a lack of enthusiasm and purpose for learning, and that's very different from poor behavior.

Reframing

It is difficult for teachers to try new strategies to improve their classrooms without seeing and thinking in new ways. One way for teachers to do this is to *reframe*. To reframe means to see something from a different perspective. The "frames" from which we see any particular situation are in large part influenced by the assumptions we bring to that situation. This means that how we make sense of that situation and any possible solutions to a problem are limited to what is within our frames. This is not limited to teaching; we can reframe situations, questions, and dilemmas all throughout our lives, such as in our family life, issues involving the environment, our habits as consumers, how we see and interact with media, our roles as citizens, and the roles of corporate America. To reframe is to open up our perspectives to choose from other, previously unimagined possible actions and solutions. Why is this a good thing to do? Here are five interconnected reasons:

- so we don't jump to conclusions and judgments, and we're willing to wait and take some time (when we can) to act

- so we don't automatically blame students if something isn't working

- to be critical of our own taken-for-granted assumptions, the larger systems, outside authorities, and dominant paradigms and belief systems

- to see and understand the complexities of our classroom dilemmas

- to consider alternative solutions to problems and injustices

When we reframe a problem we're having in the classroom, there is no guarantee that we'll either solve the problem or come up with an easier solution. In fact, many of the ideas that come from reframing are more holistic, critical, and long-term, so they can entail more work and time to implement than more traditional strategies. This is an important point because in the process of reframing we might change our original question (or dilemma), or at least come up with additional questions. This means that we need to be *prepared* to come up with new questions, expanding our inquiry to our own actions and assumptions. Being a reflective teacher is not convenient or pain-free. Reflective teaching and reframing are courageous because as teachers we're no longer limiting our views to the easiest targets (the kids, outside systems, bureaucratic policies, parents, etc.), but widening them to everyone, including ourselves.

It can help to understand reframing by applying the idea to something outside of education. Let's consider voting in the United States. Voter turnout in U.S. elections is very low. The primary elections for the 2000 presidential election had a dismal 13.6 percent turnout for Republicans and a 10.1 percent turnout for Democrats. The turnout of eligible voters for the general election barely topped 50 percent. To frame and reframe this dilemma, ask yourself these two questions: Why do so many Americans not vote? And how can we get more people to vote?

This is a question that political scientists, journalists, politicians, Washington pundits, and everyday citizens debate. It is a deeply serious problem in our country. The answer to the question that I hear so often is that people don't vote because they don't see much point in voting; they feel disenfranchised from government, they don't like or trust government, and they think it will make little difference who they vote for anyway. Now let's reframe the question and look at it from other perspectives. Here are some other possible reasons many people don't vote:

- It's harder for many poor and lower income people to get to the polls because many of them rely on public transportation.

- Many poor and lower income voters need to work two jobs or stay at home with their kids.

- Some people are lazy.

- Some people forget to register to vote and (by most existing laws) need to be registered twenty-nine days prior to the election.

- It's too tough to vote, because Election Day is a workday.

- The small and select number of major party candidates does not inspire the voters.

- The primary election process is being made shorter and shorter, limiting voter involvement and causing many candidates to drop out early.

- Some people are ignorant about the issues, the candidates, and the influence of elective office and don't realize the power voting can have.

- Some people dislike how the media report and call an election while voting is still going on.

- With Election Day in the fall, some areas of the country can have bad weather.

As you can see, there are many possible reasons we have low voter turnout, including some that I didn't come up with. All of the possibilities that I listed above came from my reframing the dilemma of low voter turnout and looking at the question from multiple perspectives. Simply stating the reason as voter apathy and disenfranchisement is far too limiting. By seeing other perspectives we also see other remedies:

- Make Election Day a national holiday.

- Add more voting precincts so low-income people can get to the polls more easily.

- Make public transportation free on Election Day.

- Permit voting on the Internet.

- Allow same-day voter registration on Election Day.

- Improve education about voting, issues, candidates, and civic participation.

- Reduce poverty.

- Change how the media covers our elections.

- Get better and more inspiring candidates to run for office.

- Lengthen the primary election process.

- Open up the monopoly of our two-party system to more political parties and candidates.

- Change how we vote for president and other offices: Instead of voting for one candidate, have "choice voting" whereby we prioritize candidates (first choice, second choice, third choice, etc.), like other democracies, such as Australia (with a typical voter turnout above 80 percent). Or have "approval voting," which allows people to vote for all the candidates they approve of, meaning they could vote "yes" for three out of seven presidential candidates. (The candidate with the most yeses wins.) Have "instant runoff voting" in which the winner must get a certain percentage of the total vote (maybe 40 percent), but if no candidate has that, the candidates with the lower votes are eliminated one at a time (and then the voter's second choice is counted).

- Have another choice on ballots: "None of the above."

- Move Election Day to the spring or summer when the weather is better.

None of these suggestions alone can solve the problem of low voter turn-out, but if we don't reframe the dilemma, then we're seriously limiting our options to solve it. (We're also not being honest. Reframing encourages us to be critical, to ask hard questions, and to look for connections, such as low voter turnout and poverty.) By reframing we open up new ways to see and new solutions to try.

Teachers can do the same in their classrooms. Here are three short examples of reframing issues of classroom management and student behavior:

1. Reframing can be as simple as how we see a student. I had a fifth grader I'll call Eric with terrible behavior. He disrupted our classroom, cracked jokes, was belligerent, and did little work. Eric and I were at odds for the entire year. But consider this point from Chandler (1998): "Don't make the assumption that students cannot change simply because they don't change. Students do behave quite differently with different teachers or in different contexts" (p. 365). As I look back this is exactly right. I saw Eric in one way: as a kid in my classroom with terrible behavior. I don't believe I considered the possibility that Eric had good behavior outside of our classroom. I'm sure that in other contexts—such as playing with his friends or watching a movie—Eric had good behavior. If I saw him through this lens, perhaps I would have asked myself what I could do to bring that good behavior out of him rather than only blame him for his bad behavior.

2. I was observing a student teacher (I'll call her Jenny) in a third-grade classroom. She was going to conduct a short lecture on the history of Chicago. Just as I had suggested in our social studies methods class, Jenny told the kids to come up to the board and sit before her. Soon they became completely disorganized and started to talk incessantly. Jenny, standing before them, continued to teach. Most of the kids were ignoring her and talking over her to each other. To Jenny, this was the students being "bad." But this was not really the kids' problem. Yes, they were misbehaving, even being rude, but Jenny set this up for problems from the start. First, she had the students bring their chairs up to sit in (instead of having them sit on the floor). The aisles between the desks weren't wide enough to do this easily, requiring the kids to push desks out of the way (and all the kids were doing this simultaneously). Once they got to the board, there wasn't enough room

for the all the kids and their chairs, so they were crammed together. By the time Jenny, started the scene was chaotic and out of control. Second, Jenny started to teach about the history of Chicago instead of first taking a few minutes to quiet them down, refocus them, and get their attention. Finally, she never stopped lecturing. She was talking about Chicago, a city these kids knew a lot about, but she never involved them. Rather than creating a relevant and meaningful interactive discussion, she delivered a lecture, which just exacerbated the chaos.

3. This story is a compilation from several different experiences and observations. A fifth-grade teacher (I'll call him Andy), liked to read novels aloud to his class. But he was frustrated because while he read many of his students goofed off and others paid little attention to him or the book. They would daydream, whisper to their classmates, play with little toys in their desks, doodle, and a few even fell asleep. No matter how much Andy spoke to his class or gave them consequences for their poor behavior, the situation did not improve. This was shocking to Andy because he always assumed that kids love to hear good stories, and he knew he was reading good books because he got recommendations from librarians and book lists. Andy's students, however, were all African American and Latino, and Andy was white. All of the books he read have white protagonists and were situated within a white, middle-class culture. Andy could reframe this by looking at the books he reads to his students and asking a few questions: Do they allow opportunities for his students to connect culturally with the story and characters? Will his students see relevance in the stories he reads aloud? Doing this was no guarantee that his students would behave or care. But by questioning his book selection and not simply the behavior of his students, he opens up other possible solutions that may not totally solve the problem but can improve it.

This Sounds Wonderful, but My Students Are Out of Control!

As I write these words a graduate teacher education student of mine, Laura, has recently begun her first year of teaching. Laura wanted to teach low-income children in an inner-city school and that's where she's working, on the south side of Chicago. Her fifth-grade students are almost entirely African American, with two being Latino (Laura is white); low income, with many living in public housing (Laura is middle-class); and almost all seriously behind academically. When Laura first started the year she was overwhelmed with terrible behavior problems. I've been spending some time in her classroom so I've seen her with her students and I've gotten to know them. She has done a remarkable job with her students in just the first four months of school. Most teachers will not have behavior problems as difficult as Laura's, but this is the reality for some teachers, so I want to address what teachers can do in response to serious behavior problems. First, here's what Laura had to say:

On the first day of school we had a class meeting, the kids made their own rules, we discussed why school is important, and filled out a questionnaire about who they are. I spoke in a pleasant tone, I smiled, I told them about my "democratic" ideas and how this was going to be their classroom and they would control their learning. This all seemed to go according to plan but what I didn't realize was how the students perceived me. The next week was hell. They walked out the first day of class with huge smiles on their faces and I walked out of class with "sucker" written on mine.

They thought I was a joke, an easy teacher. I wanted to quit after the first week. They didn't listen to me, they had no respect for my "democratic" ideas, and worst of all, they had no respect for me. Room 211 was infamous; we had fights, we were noisy, students weren't doing their homework, and yet I continued to pursue my dreams of a democratic classroom. Democracy to these students meant free time. So after the first week, I changed. I did things I never thought I would. I put names on the board, I used a conduct chart, classroom bathroom breaks were scheduled instead of "whenever nature calls," and my attitude changed. Immediately the students started to respond. I started sending notes home to parents, and I devised a punishment and reward system for behavior.

This turned [the class] around, but I was still not happy. This was not the classroom I wanted. I enjoyed more peaceful, silent reading times and more hands raised during discussion, but this was not what I had pictured for my first year of teaching. So, when I thought the students were ready I rearranged the classroom from rows to groups of five. We started with literature circles.

The biggest problem I face, even now, is the way the students treat each other. They have a difficult time getting along. The smallest, most insignificant thing can set them off, and then chaos. I constantly teach respect, citizenship, friendship, and kindness. After the twelfth week of school I am able to have classroom discussions, town meetings, and learning that comes from them. First and foremost my classroom is about respect, self-esteem, and the freedom to make mistakes. The children are allowed to voice their opinions and they are encouraged to question life, politics, rules, etc. The inner city is a much different place than I could have ever imagined. It's not the guns that scare me, it's the learned helplessness and the negativity that these students walk around with day after day. First you need to give them structure and then slowly but surely you can teach them how they fit in a nation of democracy, freedom, and responsibility.

Laura has a few suggestions for teachers working with students with serious and chronic behavior problems, particularly in urban and inner-city schools. She suggests having a structured classroom; planning your day carefully and thoroughly; learning about your students' home lives by getting to know them (possibly with interviews, surveys, or journal writing); documenting everything; giving kids lots of praise; easing your students into more democratic experiences in the classroom; and finally, she says about children: "Hug them every Friday. I hug my kids every Friday because I won't see them for two days."

These are good suggestions that I'm sure will be evolving throughout Laura's teaching career—remember, she's been teaching for only four months. I experienced some of what Laura is experiencing when I left teaching in the suburbs and started to teach in a Chicago public school. It must be honestly recognized that there are more behavior problems—and sometimes a lot more problems—in urban classrooms. However, and this must be emphasized, most of my students in my Chicago public school classrooms were well behaved and "on task." Children in low-income schools are the victims of horrendous stereotypes. Society, politicians, and the media clump together "poor" kids as the cause of those "out of control" urban classrooms. Are there more behavior and social-emotional problems in urban schools? Yes there are. But this is also where the vast majority of our poverty is located, as well as deeply underfunded schools. (As a society we reap exactly what we sow.) My experience has taught me that the behavior of the vast majority of kids in urban schools is very good, and that they come to school wanting to learn. In fact, many of my students in Chicago were the most mature and thoughtful kids I have ever taught.

Still, some teachers confront serious behavior issues, so here are my suggestions for teachers working in these classrooms (which can apply to all classrooms):

- So often our urban classrooms are culturally diverse, so teachers should strive to make their teaching "culturally relevant" (Ladson-Billings, 1994). This was my suggestion to "Andy" in the example I wrote about earlier, to make his book selection culturally relevant. (For more on culturally relevant teaching, see page 72.)

- Having a highly structured classroom need not mean having kids remain seated and silent for six hours a day. It means having routines, high expectations, well-planned teaching, and a classroom ethos that communicates intolerance of disruptive and rude behavior. Highly structured classrooms also build structure into assignments and projects, such as assignment sheets shown in Chapter 3.

- Use children's literature, especially through reading aloud. I have rarely met a kid who could not get into a good, relevant story. Reading books and stories aloud adds structure, allows the teacher to help get kids into the story, and offers endless opportunities for projects and assignments students can do about the book. For more on using literature, see Chapter 5.

- Be firm, concise, and direct, but also humane, caring, and fair.

- Start slow, take one step at a time, and work with the kids with the goal of giving them more freedom and decision making in their learning. Limit this at first. The more control and ownership we have in our learning the more we *care* about our learning.

- Invite parents into your classroom. Show them that you care about their children and ask for their help and input.

- Get others to help you: colleagues; school social workers, psychologists, and nurses; administrators; friends and peers; and gym teachers and coaches, who often have close relationships with some students (Christensen, 2000).

- Help the kids to succeed and celebrate that success. For some children in high need, classroom success can be as simple as writing a complete paragraph during journal writing. If that's growth, celebrate it.

- Have students do as much authentic work as possible that is situated in their lives and interests. Regard their lives as important and as rich as the life of any child. For example, have the class write and create a class magazine or newspaper about their neighborhood. If most of the kids only write one paragraph, accept them, honor them, edit them, and publish the magazine. If half the class doesn't turn in the writing, publish what was turned in. If it looks good, is well written, and is relevant, I'm sure the next one will be longer, better, and have more student participation.

- Have class meetings about issues of behavior in the classroom. Instead of lecturing to kids about their behavior, allow them to discuss it.

- Constantly look for opportunities to give your students decision-making power on what to learn, how to learn, and how to show what they've learned. For example, let them choose what to write about, let them pick books to read, or give them different options to show what they've learned after studying a certain topic. For example, let them write and illustrate a children's picture book on "plants," create a website, make a video, or draw a series of posters.

- Develop trusting, respectful, and caring relationships wih your students. This is one of the most underrated—and most important—dimensions of teaching. The key to building good relationships with students is taking the time to really get to know them: their lives, cultures, passions, and unique voices. Dave Brown (2002) quotes Colette, a teacher in Philadelphia: "I really believe you have to make that social and emotional connection with kids in order to get inside their heads. You have to get their heart before you get their head. The fact that you care makes them see you differently" (p. 67).

Martin Haberman (1995) has spent decades researching what he calls "star teachers of children in poverty." He has identified characteristics of successful teachers working with impoverished students. It is interesting to note that these characteristics are very close to what I am advocating in this book for *all* students. Haberman believes that these teachers "are not very concerned with discipline." This may seem surprising—perhaps the complete opposite of what we would expect—so I'll elaborate on his reasoning. This does not mean that they don't care about discipline issues, but that they have profoundly different attitudes and perspectives about them: (1) The teachers believe "problems are part of their job." They accept the complex and extremely difficult lives their students have.

(2) They don't spend a lot of time on discipline. Their normal teaching style involves much individual interaction with students. This gives them an opportunity to learn a great deal about their students before emergencies occur. These in-depth, natural interactions around classroom activities permit stars to anticipate, prevent, or ward off many emergencies. (3) Just as they expect their students to have a range of "academic" achievement, they also expect them to have a range of behaviors. (4) Haberman writes:

> The major difference between star [teachers] and other teachers is that most others . . . perceive discipline to be an issue separate from teaching. Most teachers see discipline as a set of procedures that must be put in place before learning can occur, and believe that few of their problems with discipline emanate from the way they teach. . . . The difference is between treating discipline as a prior condition and a set of controls apart from how learning activities are pursued vs. using the learning activities themselves as the basis of self-control. When students are involved in an activity, they discipline themselves. (pp. 3–6)

Classroom Values

*It is one thing to lay claim to values, to espouse
them, and quite another to try to live them out,
enact them over time in connection with others.*
                              —Robert Coles (1997)

A classroom should be built on a foundation of human and social values.
There is much controversy about teaching "values" in school. This is partly
because many people don't like teachers to teach values, saying that role
belongs in the home. However, it is impossible for teachers to *not* teach
values since everything we do is laden with values. Even if teachers are not
consciously aware of their classroom values, they still have them, because
what we value in school is what we *do* in school. And the values we espouse
are intimately connected to the politics we espouse because knowledge and
values are inherently ideological. The notion of a values-neutral (and politically neutral) school or classroom is a myth. The entire day in school is
full of values and politics, especially the knowledge we choose to teach. As
Bob Peterson (1994) writes, "Even a teacher who consciously attempts to

be politically 'neutral' makes hundreds of political decisions—from the posters on the wall to attitudes toward holidays. Is Valentine's Day celebrated, but not International Women's Day?" (p. 40). Values in school go well beyond the curriculum, including the food served in the cafeteria, whether student work is on the walls (and what kind of work it is), if the kids get recess, standardized tests, teachers' relationships with their students, classroom and school rules, if we let kids work together, and the assignments teachers give their students. These are all value statements saying, "We do this because we *value* it. This is what we believe is important." If we didn't value something, or at least see some value in it, then we wouldn't do it. We would replace it with something that we do value or that we value more. Admittedly, many teachers teach in certain ways or use certain materials because they're forced to, not because they personally value it. It's being mandated because someone somewhere values it.

The dominant value statement having to do with student behavior in schools is this: Students are behaving when they're sitting in their desks, keeping silent, listening to the teacher, and staying "on task." The values this communicates—actually *teaches* to children—include:

- The best way to learn is by sitting at a desk.

- Listening to a teacher talk is the best way to learn.

- Good learning happens when the learner remains silent.

- It's best to work alone when learning.

- Textbooks and worksheets are the best resources because they dominate the curriculum.

- You should learn without chatting to a neighbor or friend.

Are these the values of learning we want to tacitly and overtly teach to children? Many of these values are communicated to kids through the *hidden curriculum*, the daily process and rituals of school. One of the most overwhelming values traditional schooling teaches children is that learning is a passive act requiring no initiative on the part of the learner. If we valued the voice of learners as an active participant in their own learning, that's what would be happening in our classrooms.

There's nothing wrong with teaching students that there are times when we need to sit still, keep quiet, and listen, because in life there are those times (in a movie theater, during a speech, at a play or concert, even in a college lecture hall). And there's certainly value in the idea of staying on task, because we need to do that, too, in life or else we'll never get anything done and we'll be interrupting others. However, do we want to communicate that we should stay on task through external force and coercion or through intrinsic motivation and self-direction because it is the morally right and personally empowering thing to do? Forcing someone to learn is an oxymoron. I believe it was Herbert Kohl who said, "In order for the mind to comprehend the heart must first listen." His point is that the most meaningful learning happens when we are intrinsically driven to learn, to know, and to understand. When our heart chooses to listen is when we learn best. (For evidence of this consider how well you know the things that interest you the most—such as gardening or cooking or art—the vast majority of which was learned *outside* of school.)

Values have a lot in common with morals and ethics, so if the teacher is the morals model of the classroom, we can also say that the teacher is the values model of the classroom. In everything we do, teachers express value statements to our students (Fenstermacher, 1990). This includes how and what we teach, but it equally includes the relationships we develop with our students, how we speak, if and how (and why) we get angry, the "self" we present to our kids each day, and what we communicate to our students as to what is important in their lives. Imagine the different value statements two teachers can communicate to children about reading. One teacher teaches reading as if it is a "school" thing, as if it is about getting a good grade, getting into college, having good "comprehension" and "vocabulary" skills, getting high test scores, and learning to be a good reader so students can grow up and get a job. The second teacher may do all of that, but she also communicates to her kids that she *loves* reading, that being a reader is a central part of who she is, that reading brings her pleasure, that reading helps shape and improve her self and character, and that reading can help make a better world and promote democracy. The values about reading and life these two teachers teach to their students are miles apart. Perhaps the best way to nurture children to be thoughtful, lifelong learners is for their teachers to model thoughtfulness and lifelong learning. And the more our students care about their learning, the better their behavior will be.

In the context of classroom management and student behavior, teachers are behavior models. Their behavior in the classroom is a value statement, and it can teach students a lot about how they should behave. If a teacher yells at students, humiliates a student, sits at their desk a lot while the kids do "seatwork," or shows preferences toward certain students, all this can be teaching kids that these behaviors are okay. Teachers are human and they can lose their cool and get frustrated and angry (and even yell) in front of their students. (I've done all of that.) So I'm not denying the difficulty of the job or the humanness of teachers. And teachers who take time in the classroom to have children explore their behaviors are saying a lot as well. They are saying, "It is important for all of us to reflect on our behavior and to grow and improve and to think of our role in a community and to work for social justice and a better world, rather than just come to school each day and 'be good' because you'll get in trouble if you don't." Perhaps the most important classroom value is this: We must all continue to consciously work and learn throughout our lives to be the best people we can be and to use our goodness to promote a better world, and our goodness, at it's best, is never completed. We never finish being good.

The Common Good

The common good is one of the foundations of democracy and community. The common good means that we put the good of the group before the good of ourselves. I was recently talking about this idea with an undergraduate methods class and I asked them if our country honored the common good. The class laughed, overwhelmingly saying the United States has rampant individualism. How can anyone disagree with this? How often do Americans consider the good of the group before we think of the good of ourselves? Our society bombards children with the notion that "those with the most toys win." This just perpetuates a me-first society, which is the antithesis of community and acting for the common good.

To think of others should not be limited to people we know or people we have direct contact with, like our neighbors and fellow community members. The common good is an idea with no boundaries. We can think of the common good of the family and move outward to the common good of the local community, the city, state, country, and our planet. It may not seem like one person can do much for the common good of the entire planet but the truth is, they can—one-by-one, day-by-day. This is an idea that I wanted to offer my students: that for every individual who lived for the common good, the collective good was that much bigger. I've discussed this idea with my students and given them examples from history where people gave of themselves for the good of others, such as Martin Luther King, Gandhi, Mother Teresa, Myles Horton, Caesar Chavez, and Rosa Parks. But what made the Civil Rights Movement truly great wasn't King alone; it was the everyday people who joined the cause. What value would King's magnificent "I Have a Dream" speech have had if there weren't a quarter of a million people standing in front of him? Those people made it their business to be there. They were thinking of the common good.

In the classroom the common good is simple: Think and act for the good of the classroom community before the good of yourself. I did not hesitate to say this directly to my students, and to discuss it with them. I wanted them to think about that idea. I wanted to challenge them to reconceptualize why they should behave in certain ways. Typically, kids feel they need to behave because they'll get in trouble if they don't or because bad behavior will hurt their learning. I want them to consider that their poor behavior or actions hurt others and work against our classroom being a healthy and caring community. If just one student realizes that blurting out jokes in the class is good for satisfying his wants but bad for our class community, and he stops or at least improves, that's a success, and just maybe he will apply the same thinking to his life outside of school. I was visiting a classroom some years ago where the teacher gave her students a great deal of freedom. There was a sign on the wall: "With freedom comes responsibility." This teacher didn't only want to give her students freedom to learn, she wanted to use that freedom to help her students learn to be good.

Here are five ways to teach the common good, some of which will be elaborated in Chapter 4:

- Use class meetings to relate student behavior to the common good of the classroom.

- Through current events look for, discuss, and perhaps even research acts of the common good throughout the world—or example, when rich nations help poor nations; when countries help other countries after a natural disaster; or the many charitable organizations such as the Peace Corps, local tutoring programs, Habit for Humanity, and OxFam. Have students discuss and journal write on newspaper articles that expose injustices and about people working to end injustices.

- Have kids research individuals who have given much of themselves for the common good, such as Fannie Lou Hamer, Jane Addams, Lewis Hine, Septima Clark, William Lloyd Garrison, Rose Schneiderman, Nelson Mandela, and Julia Butterfly Hill (who lived in a tree for two years to stop the logging of old-growth forests).

- Students can interview people about their conceptions and practices of the common good and produce a class magazine.

- Specifically study (or at least discuss) the common good in social studies and connect it to curriculum topics and historical events, such as community, cities and states, the environment, recycling, the Women's Movement, the Civil Rights Movement, the American Indian Movement, war, the media, voting, crime, consumerism, advertising, economics, science, health care, government, and democracy.

Community

The phrase "community of learners" is trendy educational jargon. But what does *community* really mean, and is there a difference between community outside of school and community inside of school? And how can community influence students' behavior positively? What does community mean to you? Here are some words and ideas that define community to me: open, welcoming, collaborative, helpful, caring, social, compassionate, talk. I'll write about some of these ideas in more detail below, but here I'd like to look at one of them briefly: the social aspects of community.

Community cannot happen in classrooms that are not social environments. Interaction among the members of a classroom is central for community to thrive. If kids can't interact, and that includes (at times) *spontaneous* interaction, when will the qualities of community ever have an opportunity to flourish? And most important, we learn about community and being good community members by *living* community. By reflecting on our successes and failures as a community we improve our community and ourselves. A healthy community builds upon itself; it makes thoughtfulness and caring an inherent part of daily life. This can't really happen in a classroom without regular social interaction, and that means movement and talking by the students, most of which is done within the purposeful contexts of learning.

A classroom community will not happen by magic. Many educators believe that if they have kids work together in groups, they're "doing" community. But teachers can have a lot of collaborative learning going on and have no community at all. As teachers, community is not really something that we *do*; it's not a "method." Community is more a way of life and habits of mind. It most certainly is reinforced by what teachers choose for their students to do and learn about. A teacher can't "do community" like they might "do spelling," but community can't exist unless a teacher does certain things and teaches specific ideas to promote and live community. In a sense a teacher teaches the underlying values of community—such as the common good—in the hope that the students will join in. But you can't package community. It needs to be born out of each classroom as a unique environment. Here are ten ways to teach and live community:

- Read good examples of community in children's literature (see Chapter 5).

- Have kids write about community (what it means to them, good and bad examples, etc.) in their journals and discuss it.

- Talk about specific problems of community you're having in the classroom or in the local neighborhood or have a debate on a community issue, such as gun control, the sale of liquor and cigarettes, or solutions for the homeless.

- Do a research project on an actual community controversy or have the kids write and give a survey to the public on community issues. (Ask local residents: "What can we do to make our community better?")

- Write and publish a classroom newspaper that covers the classroom community.

- Maintain a large list on the wall of "Great Acts of Community" that kids have done in your classroom.

- Have regular class meetings and town meetings to discuss communal issues, problems, and successes (see Chapter 4).

- Have class parties and free time.

- Collect, discuss, and post newspaper articles that are good examples of healthy community and the common good.

- Have a word wall with words associated with community.

Empathy, Compassion, and Caring

Empathy, compassion, and caring are three of the most universal human qualities. These can be seen at the local level and the global level, from neighbors watching out for one another to nations around the world coming to the aid of a country after a devastating earthquake. These same qualities are essential for a healthy democracy. Where would our society and our country be without people caring for one another and without the ability and willingness to put themselves in another person's shoes? Yet, how often do children have opportunities in school to learn about empathy and caring? It seems the only time these values are a part of an official curriculum is in kindergarten. Flip through a social studies textbook and you will not find any mention of being empathetic to the oppressed peoples of the past and the present (women, children, the poor, cultural "minorities," laborers, etc.), or to the victims (past and present) of war, greed, ego, and the abuse of power. In fact, social studies textbooks are devoid of human emotion. Studying history and society is the perfect time to explore empathy and compassion, and yet, most official curriculums avoid the issue. Arthur Foshay (1997) in his article, "Social Studies and Emotion," writes:

> To this day, we in education imply an ideal person w,ho is unemotional—who is completely rational at all times; who is cool, even cold; who is so much in control of him or herself that no emotion is ever evident. We seek only to control the emotions, when we ought to acknowledge them as an essential part of the human condition. (p. 315)

Nel Noddings (1992) believes that "caring" should be the foundation of school curriculums. She argues that our schools should establish as one of their primary goals the teaching (and living) of caring for family, friends, strangers, plants, animals, the earth, ourselves, and ideas. Noddings also advocates teaching children to care about objects, not for materialistic ends, but more for a caring that "produces fine objects and takes care of them." She continues:

> In a society apparently devoted to planned obsolescence, our children have few opportunities to care lovingly for old furniture, dishes, carpets, or even new bicycles, radios, cassette players, and the like. It can be argued that the care of many tools and instruments is a waste of time because they are so easily replaced. But one wonders how long a throwaway society can live harmoniously with the natural

environment and also how closely this form of carelessness is related to the gross desire for more and more acquisitions. Is there a role for schools to play in teaching care of building blocks, books, computers, furniture, and laboratory equipment? (p. 20)

Helping kids to care, even about tools, blocks, and bikes, can develop their character and encourage them to be good. I have written in the past on how teachers can use poetry to encourage their students to care (Wolk, 1994). Good poetry is alive with the poets' caring for images, words, language, experiences, form, and the details of life. I wrote, "Poetry can help kids to see that there is more to life than VCRs and Nikes" (p. 89). Teaching caring isn't about lecturing to students, but rather modeling caring, discussing and debating it, looking for its presence in and absence from our lives. Here are five more ideas for teaching empathy, caring, and compassion:

- Maintain a Caring Wall in the classroom with articles, pictures, images, poems, and words having to do with caring.

- Be a model for caring. Show students that you care about learning, reading, thinking, the planet, ideas, history, math, writing, the arts, drama, and science, and share your hobbies and interests.

- Read books specifically with themes of caring and empathy. And read primary sources: personal narratives, poetry, memoirs, speeches, diaries and journals. (See Chapter 5.)

- Use "caring" words and language with your students. Don't hesitate to complement a student by saying, "Leticia, I really appreciate how empathetic you were with Amanda."

- Allow, even encourage, emotions to be a part of your classroom. Educate your students' affective selves. Talk about emotions, be honest about emotions, and promote the emotions as a central part of being human.

Thoughtfulness

When teachers help their students be more thoughtful they are helping to make their students be good. Thoughtfulness is a value statement about how we spend our time. Being thoughtful means that we consciously choose to take time to think and reflect and to consider alternative possibilities. It

means we *value* that time and that process and purpose. What value statement is our nation (and our homes) making when our televisions are on
an average of six hours per day? That is how so many Americans are
choosing to spend their time. Of course, even if we spend time being
thoughtful, it also depends on what we're thinking about. That, too, is a
value statement. So, teachers encouraging students to be thoughtful isn't
enough; they need to help them to be thoughtful about ideas that are important and educative.

Thoughtfulness can reach this deeper "level" if teachers value *intellec-
tualism* in their classroom. This is one of the greatest failures—and deep-
est ironies—of our schools. Far too often classrooms are anti-intellectual
environments. At the risk of being simplistic, to be intellectual means to
take the time to learn and reflect consciously about important things and
ideas, and to seek out (and learn from) multiple perspectives and sources.
Sadly, being an "intellectual" is a pejorative label in our society. You run
the risk of being called a "know-it-all" or a "nerd" or arrogant or a snob.
Don't we want children (and adults) to take time to think about important ideas? And a child doesn't need to be older to be intellectual. You can
have an intellectual kindergarten classroom. Here are five ways to create
a more thoughtful and intellectual classroom:

- Make intellectual topics and issues an important part of your classroom. Don't teach "down" to kids; they are capable of thinking about
  complex issues and ideas. This can be done with the youngest of children; you just need to make it at their level and relevant to their realities. Even with primary-age children you can discuss topics such as
  poverty, pollution, prejudice, the common good, community, caring,
  war, conflict, having opinions, being informed, anger, peace, equality,
  violence, goodness, and social justice.

- Help students make connections between intellectual ideas and their
  own lives. The more relevant and meaningful our experiences are, the
  more successful our learning will be. All of the ideas I mentioned
  above can be related to and situated within the lives of every human
  being. Have students write and talk about how certain intellectual
  ideas—such as conflict or prejudice—connect to their own lives.

- Help students see the thoughtfulness and curiosity in people throughout history.

- Bring people who live thoughtful and intellectual lives into your classroom to speak. Have students interview them. Help students to see that we don't have to be professors or scientists to be intellectual— anyone can be.

- Take field trips to "intellectual" places beyond the more typical field trips. In my town of Chicago, for example, there is the Peace Museum, Mexican Fine Arts Museum, Newberry Library, Oriental Institute, the *Chicago Tribune*, DuSable Museum, the Children's International Film Festival, the Chicago Mercantile Exchange, and endless events such as poetry readings, exhibits, and children's plays.

Integrity

I love the word *integrity*. While it's closely associated with honesty, it means more. People, systems, schools, and classrooms that have integrity have a moral and ethical vision of their purpose, do not sway from that vision, and strive to make it an integral part of their entire being. People with integrity do not pick and choose where to be moral and good; their acts are selfless and "pure" and focused on the common good. Classrooms and teachers that strive to be good have integrity. The important point of integrity is not to always have this pure goodness (which is rare, if not impossible), but to consciously strive toward it.

Most people would agree that teachers should be honest and encourage their students to be honest, but most people would not advocate that teachers present their true selves to their students. Teachers are advised not to share details of their private lives, to keep a certain distance from their students. But this helps create a kind of dishonest relationship between teachers and their students. By presenting themselves as complete and real human beings, teachers bring integrity to their work. Too often teachers wear a "teacher's mask," leaving the rest of their lives at home (Rogers, 1969). Many teachers believe that they should not bring their personal selves into the classroom to interfere with their professional selves. But when it comes to teaching, the personal is the professional. They are one. By presenting ourselves honestly as complete and complex people who have lives outside of school, just like kids, teachers help to nurture a relationship built upon connections that are relevant to being human. When it comes to life, teachers and their students have a lot in common. We all have emotional times of our lives, sad times and joyous times, passions, hobbies, celebrations, successes, and failures. By sharing some of these life experiences with students, teachers are being more honest; they are bringing integrity to the idea of being human, and that can help all people to be good.

Teachers need integrity in what they teach, too. Much of the official curriculums (actually the textbooks) are filled with misinformation, distortions, biased and incorrect information, and narrow and Eurocentric perspectives (especially in the social sciences and, in particular, American History). James Loewen (1994) calls our U.S. history textbooks "Disney history." Most science curriculums lack critical perspectives, and ethical, moral, and political perspectives on the sciences, technology, industry, and the environment. Teachers can bring integrity to what they teach by keeping critically informed, continually learning and reading, using resources outside the textbook, and by teaching for critical literacy

Critical Literacy

Critical literacy redefines what it means to be a "literate" human being. Traditionally, to be literate has meant to have basic skills in reading, writing, and math. Advocates of critical literacy believe that is not truly a literate person. To be critically literate means to see beneath surface realities and bias, to question taken-for-granted assumptions, to live a life of skepticism, to see oneself as an active participant in governance and social change. Critical literacy is about issues of power: who has it, who is denied it, how do people get it, how do people lose it, who abuses it, and taking action against the people, institutions, and hegemonies that use their power to oppress others. Critically literate people are especially "awake" to issues of culture and racism, economics and poverty, and gender and sexism, all in an ongoing effort to see new possibilities for making the world better, more humane, and socially just. Joseph Kretovics (1985) offers a concise definition of critical literacy as:

> providing students not merely with functional skills, but with the conceptual tools necessary to critique and engage society along with its inequalities and injustices. Furthermore, critical literacy can stress the need for students to develop a collective vision of what it might be like to live in the best of all societies and how such a vision might be made practical. (p. 87)

Critical literacy can do at least five things: empower us to be in control; enlighten us to be informed; encourage us to ask questions; nurture in us the will to act for a better world; and help us to look inward and be critical of *ourselves* and how we see the world. Put all of these ideas together and one of the common threads is goodness. Helping children explore life and knowledge from a critical perspective is helping them to ask questions about what is good and just and morally right. It is teaching kids to think for themselves, grapple with complex issues, take stances on how they want to live their lives, and to have the civic courage to act for change and social justice. Here are nine ways to teach for critical literacy:

1. Bring at least one good newspaper to class every day. Read the paper and have students write about issues in the news. (See Chapter 4)
2. Have kids talk about, write about, and debate such issues as power, prejudice, democracy, and equality, and help them to see how these are a part of our lives on a daily basis.
3. Help students to be critical of the knowledge and perspectives in their textbooks. Bring into the classroom the voices that are typically silenced in society: the poor, women, culturally diverse places and people, labor groups. This can be done through children's literature, poems, videos, newspapers, and class visitors.
4. Explore, research, and debate governmental policies and laws.
5. Study how we interact with and use the media (and how the media uses us). Compare newspaper articles to the same stories on television news.
6. Expand kids' research assignments. When studying scientists or historical figures, have them research women and people from a variety of cultures. Go beyond researching presidents and have them learn about social activists, environmentalists, labor leaders, philosophers, writers, poets, and artists.
7. Make your classroom highly multicultural and specifically teach an anti-racist and anti-oppression curriculum.
8. Model being critically literate. Let your students see you being critical of knowledge, social assumptions, and dominant perspectives.
9. Pull critical ideas and themes out of children's literature. Connect these themes to the lives of your students. (See Chapter 5.)
10. Have kids conduct interviews and surveys on people's opinions of and experiences with critial issues, such as economics and poverty,

prejudice, the environment, consumerism, and so on. Have kids write and publish interviews and graph surveys.

Equality

Can equality exist in a classroom? The teacher must be the final authority in the classroom, which means that teachers will have more power than students. However, teachers and students can be equal in that all are human beings. At the human level we are all equal. In a classroom context this means that teachers must respect their students as complete and complex people and see them each day as having those same fundamental rights. It means that teachers need to see their students as human beings. They need to value their students' ideas, opinions, perspectives, life experiences, cultures, existing knowledge, theories of how the world works, and their unique understandings and meanings. Consider for a moment our life experiences. Are any of my life experiences more important than the life experiences of an eight-year-old? When I was teaching elementary school my students had had experiences that I did not have. That means I could learn things from them. That means I need to value their experiences as equal to my own.

Valuing equality in our classrooms can help kids explore their own sense of equality. The topic can be a part of a classroom curriculum. Do children, for example, believe we have equality in our country? Do they consider all of the kids in their school to be equal? Are the "popular" kids equal to the "unpopular" kids? Do the "jocks" get special treatment? All of these questions are ripe for students to explore, such as through journal writing and class discussion. When kids see themselves as being equal in these human terms, they develop better relationships.

Quality

There are many ways people can have or produce quality. You can refinish an old piece of furniture with quality. You can cut your lawn with quality. You can raise a child with quality. You can eat with quality. You can think in quality ways. Being good is also a quality. Quality can be a goal in performing a play on community in second grade, playing the trombone in the fourth-grade orchestra, researching the plight of African elephants for a fifth-grade project, and growing lima bean plants for a science experiment in seventh grade. When people do any of these things with quality they are practicing goodness, because producing quality and striving for quality is being good.

By teaching quality it becomes a value in a classroom. The value statement teachers are saying to their students is, "Our classroom is about creating quality in our selves, in our learning, in our classroom community." Sadly, I don't see much quality in classrooms. I'm in classrooms all the time and what I see far more often are teachers and kids in a big rush to finish what they're working on so they can move on to the next thing. This teaches the opposite of quality. It makes hastiness and thoughtlessness the value in a classroom, not reflection and excellence. Teachers can help their students see the connection between a high-quality play they performed and the high quality of their behavior on a field trip. Both have goodness.

Quality takes time, and that's something many educators don't think they have. But teaching quality should not be done as a separate "subject." It can be imbedded into all that students do. For example, whenever my students were working on a project, such as creating board games based on what they learned about the American Revolution, or poster-board graphs from data they collected from surveys on social issues (Wolk, 1998), I had them make small draft versions first. And usually they would spend weeks (sometimes many weeks) on that smaller version, refining it, making it the best it could be. Once the small-sketched version was done, they moved on to the final version, which they had to do in pencil first for editing ease. By going through this process I was teaching—and valuing— quality, and I was using that language, not hesitant at all to say "quality" and point out examples of it. This is the same philosophy I expected (and taught) in writing and reading workshop: to have my students put a lot of time and thought into their writing and reading; to care about it. When we care about something we are more than willing to put time into it, and that's being good. Here are five more ways to promote and teach quality:

- Have all students' publishable writing go through a writing process. Have all kids first self-edit their writing, possibly have a peer edit, and do a final teacher edit; have the students create a final copy, and then do a final proofread. All finished, publishable, final writing (across the curriculum) should be flawless.

- Teach students how to create quality in their work. For example, show them how to draw straight, parallel, and perpendicular lines for projects. Have them do certain work, such as creating a poster or writing and illustrating a children's book, as a small copy first.

- Give kids lots of time to do their work. Teach them that quality requires time and effort. Many of my students' projects took four to seven weeks to complete.

- Have kids do most of their work in class when you can help them.

- Model quality for your students. Show them previous students' work and, at times, do some of the work, too, and share it with your students. When students see quality, they want to produce quality themselves.

Voice

To value voice means to value individuality. It is a way to celebrate uniqueness and diversity and the freedom to express that diversity. Valuing voice is equally about helping students to shape their minds. At its best, voice is not empty or neutral; it is filled and fueled by passion and commitment and our own personal values and ideologies. Many educators (including myself) have been critical that school so rarely allows children to talk or to ask and explore an original question. Even more serious is the rarity of encouraging—actually teaching—children to consciously form their "self," which is exactly what gives their voices shape and identity. If we want children (and later adults) to think for themselves, then we must make developing voice a central purpose and experience of going to school.

Of course, along with expressing and sharing our voices comes responsibility and decision making. First, people need to be responsible for what they say, write, and communicate. We must understand that words and images can hurt people. How this relates to student behavior in the classroom is obvious. Our voices don't exist in a vacuum; they're part of a larger world. We need to honor the power of our voices and understand that words can hurt. The old saying, "Sticks and stones may break my bones but names will never hurt me" is simply untrue.

Second, as we develop our voices we make moral choices, some consciously and some unconsciously, about what values will give them shape. Classrooms can be a place for children (and teachers) to shape their "moral identities" (Glover, 1999). Classrooms can be fertile "public spaces" (Adler, 2000; Greene, 1988) to help kids examine those values that form their voices. The purpose is not to tell children what to think. When I taught elementary and middle school I didn't tell my students which values or opinions they should adopt. I wanted to encourage them *to* think. Of course I *influenced* their decision making simply by choosing and expanding the knowledge I allowed in our classroom. *All* teachers influence their students, but usually within narrower parameters, ultimately limiting their decision-making options. If we can't imagine an option, then we can't choose an option.

The big idea here is to teach that how we choose to live our lives is in essence a value statement and an extension of our voice or our "self." Every day we're constantly making decisions and choices, including kids. Those decisions—seen in how we act—are saying, "I believe this" or "I like this" or "This is good." Every child knows what it means to be "picked on." But the choice an individual student makes to join or not to join a group of kids at recess that's picking on another student is a moral choice, and that is a reflection of our self and a question of goodness. Teachers can help their students make those decisions, or perhaps even more importantly, encourage their students to *think about* their decisions.

Here are ten ways to help kids share and develop their voices, some of which have been mentioned before:

1. Class discussions
2. Journal writing
3. Debates
4. Newspaper reading
5. Writing and performing plays and skits
6. Read and write memoirs, personal narratives, and poetry, which are often about the authors' self and voice. Give kids regular opportunities to write about and talk about what they believe and to listen to what others believe.
7. Read and write children's literature and poetry.
8. Research controversial issues and take positions. Make creativity and imagination an important part of your classroom. Allow children to use many mediums and "intelligences" to show what they have learned and to communicate their opinions and ideas. Engage your students in drama, the visual arts, photography, computer multimedia, writing, model building, music, dance, and hands-on science experiments. By allowing your students to be creative you are allowing

them (actually helping them) to develop and connect with their unique selves.

9. Give students the freedom to write what they want to write and read the books they want to read. This can be done by having a reading and writing workshop (Atwell, 1998). Children can be given this freedom within some limits and specific expectations.

10. Create a peer mediation program in your school or classroom. This allows your students to have a voice and role in solving conflicts among students.

Freedom

Many people feel freedom should be the last value in a classroom, but I think it should be one of the first. Right now the highest value that much of our society puts on our schools is test scores. But what difference does it make how highs a test score is if people don't have the skills, and courage to freely think for themselves, the passion to express their views, and the interest in working to make the world a better place? From the day children first enter school they are told what to study, how to study, and when to study. They are told that their job as a student is primarily to be quiet, to sit still, to pay attention, and to do as they are told. As I explained in Chapter 1, these daily rituals in school are the hidden curriculum, and it is a powerful force in shaping lifelong attitudes and habits of mind in students. Children learn to be passive, and passivity is the opposite of freedom, as it instills in children (and later, adults) complacency, civic apathy, and a void of creativity and critical literacy.

As teachers we must confront the issues of freedom in our classrooms according to our own comfort zones, our beliefs and philosophies, and what is explicitly and implicitly allowed at our schools. While some teachers are open to more freedoms, other teachers need (or want) more structure and control. Here are five points to keep in mind about freedom and control:

1. This is not an either–or situation; it is not deciding between a class-room with complete freedom or a classroom with complete control. The range between freedom and control is a never-ending continuum with endless variations in between.

2. A teacher's decision about where his or her classroom falls on that

continuum should not be finite; these decisions should be evolving. A freedom that you may not want to implement in September you may be excited about trying out in January.

3. Many people confuse the idea of freedom in the classroom with the notion of "lack of structure" or "no order." These are *not* synonymous. A classroom can have freedom, even a lot of freedom, and still have structure and order.

4. Most adults assume that without a rigidly controlled classroom the students will run amok and not learn anything. While different children may need varying degrees of control, that assumption begins with a lack of trust in children. And kids who need more structure in September usually require less structure in November, especially in classrooms about being good.

5. Freedom is not just a "method" to implement. It can be a part of the classroom curriculum. By living freedom with all of its messy complexity, teachers can help children understand that with freedom comes responsibility and the necessity of varying limitations.

Teachers can make freedom a part of their classrooms in many ways and to widely varying degrees. They can allow their students to choose their own books to read and their own topics to write about through reading and writing workshops. Students can engage in open discussion and debate through class meetings and journal writing. They can let students choose their own sub-topic to study from a larger unit or project, such as allowing one student to research African art and another to research endangered African wildlife in a unit on Africa. Teachers can give kids blocks of time—periodically or even one hour a day—to let them study what they want to learn about (see Wolk, 2002). Classrooms based on multiple intelligences (Gardner, 1983) value freedom because the theory is based on the belief that all people are different and have different strengths and interests. So teachers can allow their students to choose different ways of showing what they've learned. For example, for the project on Africa one student can write a play, another can write and illustrate a children's book, another can build a model, and another can create a mural. Teachers can also free students by assessing them individually and authentically, rather than holding them to a universal "fifth grade standard" that is based on the belief that all ten-year-olds are alike. Kids can also be given the freedom to sit where they want, go to the bathroom and get a drink of water when they want, and engage in spontaneous talk while they work. Freedom comes in all shapes and sizes, and one size does not fit all teachers or all students.

A Final Thought: Classroom Rules

Having some kind of classroom "rules" has become a staple inside our schools. It is possible for teachers to have "classroom values" rather than (or addition to) some kind of explicit classroom rules. Classroom values, as opposed to rules, emphasize what is good and desirable rather than what is bad and forbidden. If teachers like this idea, I'd suggest that they discuss and write the classroom values with their students. This could even be a bigger project. Imagine a class creating murals based on the following classroom values and hanging them up all around the classroom, or writing and performing short skits:

Our Classroom Values

- Peace and nonviolent conflict resolution

- Mutual respect

- Thoughtfulness

- Empathy and expressing our feelings

- Caring for ideas, people, and other living things

- Appreciating our differences

- Meaningful learning

- Community, the common good, and working for social justice

- Developing our unique voices and passions

- Thinking for ourselves

Some Practical Suggestions 3

> *In saying that a classroom is a "community," then,*
> *I mean that it is a place in which students feel*
> *cared about and are encouraged to care about each*
> *other. They experience a sense of being valued and*
> *respected; the children matter to one another and*
> *to the teacher. They have come to think in the*
> *plural: they feel connected to each other; they are*
> *part of an "us."*
>
> — Alfie Kohn (1996)

Whichever form of classroom management a teacher chooses to practice, either more traditional or more democratic, there are some practical and logistical ideas that can help. If you like some of them, try them out and see how they work. But remember that for a strategy to work well (or at least have some success) it usually requires a fair amount of time, and in some cases that can mean months. If an idea isn't working well, don't automatically toss it out; all it may need is an adjustment. If after a fair amount of time you don't see any benefits, consider how you might improve it. Sometimes the slightest change can be the difference between failure and success.

Create Classroom Community

At its best, community is about how we act and treat other people. By promoting, teaching, and *living* community, we are actually teaching compassion, empathy, thoughtfulness, the common good, democracy, acceptance, tolerance, diversity, working together, and being good. These are the qualities that make a healthy and caring community. Many of the ideas in this chapter can help teach these qualities. Perhaps the simplest way to teach them is to spend a lot of time talking about them with your students—and helping the kids to do most of the talking. By engaging kids in open and intellectual discussion about the qualities of community, teachers are encouraging their students to think about what community means to them and the people they want to be. As I'll elaborate in the next chapter, these discussions can be one of many parts of a classroom curriculum: newspaper articles, the media (music, movies, videogames), the kids' own lives, children's literature, required school topics (the American Civil War, life science, writing, etc.). Talking about a character's empathy (or lack of it) in a children's novel, about a bad (or good) situation in a student's life, or a newspaper article on a corporation that is abusing the environment can promote community, connectedness, and responsibility.

Getting to Know Your Students

In Chapter 1 I wrote about the importance of developing caring, trusting, and respectful relationships with students, and that one of the best ways to do this is to really get to know each of your kids. Getting to know your students as unique people with different cultures, families, interests, opinions, and life experiences is also one of the best ways to create classroom community. Having good relationships with your students, knowing them, and having a healthy community in your classroom can help to dramatically decrease problems with student behavior, as well as help resolve problems peacefully when you do have them. Here are ten ways to get to know your students:

1. Give kids disposable cameras to take home (or have them rotate using regular cameras). Have them take pictures of things that are important to them; develop the pictures; and then have them write about, share, and discuss their pictures (s ee Allen et al., 2002). Hang the pictures around the room to celebrate them.

2. Invite your students' parents and siblings to your class for a "family day" and share food, stories, cultures, and learning. Invite families to your classroom and have your students share their schoolwork with them.

3. Have kids create what I call *life graphs* (Reif, 1992). Draw two axes so they look like a sideways capital "T" (with the top of the "T" on the left). On the vertical line above the horizontal line write +1, +2, +3, +4, +5, and below the line write −1, −2, −3, −4, −5. On the horizontal line write 1, 2, 3, and so on, until you reach your students' ages. Then have kids make two lists: good experiences/events and bad experiences/events from throughout their lives. Have them include their age when it happened. Then have them rate each experience on how good and how bad it was, with +5 being the best (such as "My baby sister was born.") and −5 being the worst (such as "My grandma died."). Have kids plot each item on their graphs in chronological order and connect the dots with straight lines. To finish the graph, have the kids write what event each dot represents and perhaps draw a tiny picture or symbol next to it. Sit in a circle and share them. (The teacher should make one, too.)

4. Have students learn about, write about, and share their family histories and stories. Also have kids write and publish their autobiographies. Bob Peterson (1994) does this for the first six weeks of each school year. This is a wonderful way to communicate to kids right from the start that their classroom is not really about textbooks and tests but rather it's about *us*.

5. Encourage (or assign) students to write personal narratives. (Some of these can come from the items listed on their life graphs.)

6. Have kids collect data about their lives and create a *Graph Autobiography*. They can collect data on how they spend their time, what they buy, what they eat, what they watch on TV, what they own, and so forth. Have kids survey one another in the class (favorite TV shows, favorite authors, favorite music, etc.) and have kids make large poster-board graphs and display them around the classroom.

7. Have kids read a novel that connects to their lives in some way (through culture, economic class, the characters, the setting, the plot, etc.).
8. Have students find a picture book that reminds them of their life, family, culture, experiences, and so forth, in some way. Let one student read their book aloud to the class each week and lead a class discussion about it. Beforehand, have the student write some good questions to start the discussion and explain his or her connection to the book to the class. I did something similar to this with fourth and fifth graders called "Friday Picture Book Day" (Wolk, 1998).
9. Have regular class meetings where you ask your students what is happening in their lives.
10. Have kids write and illustrate picture books about their neighborhoods.

Let Scheduling Help You

How teachers schedule their day can help with issues of student behavior. I liked to begin every day with a morning meeting. At the start of each day my students entered our classroom, set their things down, and sat in a circle on our large rug. I sat with them on the rug. The greatest benefit of morning meetings is that we started each day together, as a community in a circle, facing each other. (Having a morning meeting with the kids in their desks would have taken much away from this time. Sitting on the floor was important. If I couldn't have a rug or I didn't have space to sit on the floor in a circle, I would probably put the desks in a circle for class meetings.) Another benefit is helping to calm and focus the kids at the start of each day, and this was particularly useful when I began to teach in a Chicago public school, where many of my students were on a noisy and bumpy school bus for an hour. Our morning meetings helped put my students in a better frame of mind to work productively and thoughtfully.

Morning meetings also allowed me to help my students think about their behavior and learning for the day. I had a class of third and fourth graders a few years ago that particularly struggled with their behavior on Mondays. After a long weekend of playing and TV and telephones and junk food, many of the kids came to school on Monday pumped with energy. Once I realized this I started to talk about it at our Monday morning meetings. I said, "Remember, today is Monday. Mondays are tough for us. Many of you have some trouble with your self-control on Mondays, so we all need to think before we act, we need to all be our best, and we need to work together."

I was also careful about what I scheduled after lunch, recess, and gym. All of these are like that bumpy bus ride. They're all important, allowing kids time to socialize and play (which is a powerful learning time) and burn off energy, but they also send kids back into a classroom sweaty and chatty and huffing and puffing. I tried to schedule our daily thirty- to forty-minute quiet reading time (what some call SSR or DEAR) right after one of these. The kids knew that as they entered the classroom they had to get their book, find a comfortable place, and read silently. This gave everyone some quiet time to settle down.

One of the most important points on scheduling is how long kids are made to sit. I visit classrooms a lot, and in most of these rooms the students are sitting all day. Is it any wonder they get antsy? Is it any wonder they have behavior problems? Is it any wonder their minds wander? Because of this, when I taught I broke up our more "sitting" parts of the day with our more active parts of the day. If we had writing workshop (which is primarily sitting and working on self-chosen writing) for an hour right after our morning meeting (where we also sat, but on the floor), we would then have an hour project time to work on a long-term project (for example, a social studies project), which usually involved a lot of free movement. And even within those sitting parts of the day, such as writing workshop, students were not nailed to their seats for an entire hour, which can cause kids (and adults) to lose focus. They were free to get up and confer or collaborate with others on their writing; they were free to get supplies from our supply area, sharpen a pencil, go to the bathroom, or get a drink of water. (The amount of freedom they were given depended on how much freedom they could responsibly handle.) There certainly are times for sitting quietly in a classroom, but people are *social animals*, so our human biology tells us—and especially kids—to *move* and to *talk*, so we need to give students productive ways to do that throughout the day, which will help them to be good.

How I planned the end of our school day also helped with issues of student behavior. Just like adults, kids get tired as the day wears on. I don't blame kids for losing some focus and energy as the clock ticks toward two o'clock; after all, I'm tired, too. I tried to schedule certain things for the last few hours of the day that had a better chance of keeping the kids interested and focused. For example, I had another math or science project time late in the day to keep the kids active. Keeping students glued to their desks for the last two hours of the day is a good way to put them to sleep and invite poor behavior. They're already tired, exacerbating the problem. So I avoided having quiet reading time, lengthy lectures, or direct instruction in the last two hours of the day; and I tried to have at least one more active time during the later afternoon. I usually had a class meeting for the last thirty minutes of each day, which was similar to our morning meetings (see Chapter 4).

I put a lot of thought into how I scheduled my days, and it was constantly evolving. Routines can definitely help kids. Coming up with an overall schedule and sticking with it so the students get into a routine is important, not only for good behavior, but also for good learning. However, I also believe that it's important for teachers to regularly reflect on their schedule and be willing to make changes and experiment. While too many changes can hinder helping kids to be good, trying a new scheduling idea can open up new possibilities.

Give Responsibility

Giving students responsibilities can improve their behavior. This can be especially true for kids with chronic behavior problems. And the more genuine and meaningful responsibility people (not only kids) are given, the more pride they feel in their work and in how they live and get along with others. Giving kids responsibilities is also a way to teach them the value of community and the common good. It's not just about having a student pass out papers to save the teacher time. It's also about communicating to your students that people who live in a caring community help each other and contribute to the good of the group. Some of the responsibilities I've given my students include having a student take attendance every morning during our morning meeting (showing it to me before taking it down to the office); having "travelers" pass out journals, research folders, and other items to their table or group; having kids tutor and read to other kids, including younger students in other classes; having students rotate being class librarian, maintaining our class library; and having students take care of our classroom plants.

Give Some Thought to Seating

There are two big issues with seating: how desks or tables will be arranged and where students will sit. For most of the history of American schooling kids sat in rows facing the front of the room, the teacher's desk, the chalkboard, and the teacher standing before them. In fact, most teachers didn't have a choice since the students' desks were bolted to the floor. The reason for this seating arrangement can be summed up in one word: control. With all of the kids facing forward in rows and not near each other, the teacher could maintain control. Of course, this didn't (and still doesn't) mean the students were learning anything or were intellectually engaged; it just meant they were under the teacher's watchful eyes.

This Victorian schoolroom has slowly changed. More and more teachers are pushing desks together and letting their kids sit in groups of four or five. Other teachers are getting rid of individual desks and replacing them with tables. My students sat together in either groups of desks or at tables. I also arranged my classrooms in such a way as to have a large open space with a rug or carpeting for various purposes, such as class meetings, student performances, work areas, and quiet reading time. How students' desks are arranged influences student behavior. Part of this arrangement depends on what the kids can handle. As mentioned, historically desks have been in rows. For teachers who want to get away from that, there are different arrangement possibilities. Desks can be pushed together in small groups. They can be arranged in a large U-shape or in two large L's that form a rectangle but have openings in two corners (in both of the latter two plans the inside space can be used for a large rug). If students can't work well sitting in groups, then teachers can set that as a goal. In Chapter 1 my graduate student, Laura, wrote about her difficulties with her fifth graders. They couldn't handle sitting in groups at the start of the year, so she put them in rows. But she worked with them on behavior and community with the specific goal of moving them into groups as soon as they were ready. After six weeks she moved their desks together and that's how they have remained.

There are many people who would still say that group seating arrangements are exactly what *shouldn't* be done if you want kids to behave. But this is a Victorian assumption: if you put kids together they'll misbehave. Having kids work together should be about more than just the "academic" content you want them to learn. When students sit together it is the perfect opportunity to help kids learn *how* and *why* to sit and work *together*—and those are issues of behavior, character, control, power, and responsibility. Laura didn't see her seating arrangement as just about having her kids sit, but as a way to help her kids learn to be good and live as a community. Of course, when kids sit together there can be some behavior problems (chit-chat, boundary issues, arguments, being off task). But as a teacher I accepted these "smaller" problems because of my bigger purpose of helping my students develop self-control and work well with others.

The second seating issue is how a teacher decides where each student will sit. I don't remember ever being allowed to choose my own seat when I was in school. Assigning students a desk or seat is one of the unquestioned assumptions of being a teacher. Most teachers do it without thinking about alternatives. Allowing kids the freedom to choose their own seat, however, is a great opportunity to have them think about responsibility and behavior. I began each school year letting my students choose where to sit. But I also used that to teach them that with freedom comes responsibility, and if they did not have the responsibility they would lose that freedom. I would say to the class something like this:

> I'm giving you this freedom because I trust you. Coming to school is not about hanging out with your friends and chatting about last night's basketball game. We're here to work hard and take our learning seriously. If you believe you can do that while sitting with your friends, then you're free to do that. But if you can't, then I strongly suggest you choose to sit with someone else. If your seating choice disrupts your learning or another student's learning, I'll move you to an assigned seat. Think about this carefully and then make a decision.

Did this always work? No! It depended on the class and the individual kids. Some years were better than others. But it *did* work for some kids right away, and most of the others accepted the responsibility over time. I've also had a handful of students that it never worked for, so I assigned them a seat. My bigger goal with seating issues was to use them to help my students learn about making good decisions and being good. Later in my teaching I added one stipulation to my students' self-chosen seating: They had to sit in mixed-gender and mixed-ethnicity groups to promote community and tolerance. I would make any necessary changes to ensure heterogeneous groups. Given these limits, this assigned seating process was more a collaboration between the students and me than a sit-wherever-you-want freedom. I talked about this with my class, explaining my thinking and inviting their feedback. Some of them didn't care, some of them liked it, and a few of them hated it, but they all did it without any argument, in part because I took the time to talk about it and let them voice their opinions, even if they disagreed with mine. Finally, I agree with Bob Peterson (1994), who rearranges his student groups every nine weeks. This promotes community and helps students to make new connections. If I were teaching now I would tell my students that they will have to change their groups four times a year—after each term—and sit with new people.

Reduce Clutter, Be Organized, and Honor Kids' Work

A cluttered space is a cluttered mind. I've been in classrooms that had enormous amounts of clutter—stuff stacked on shelves and counters or piled on tables and windowsills; every inch of wall covered with posters on verbs, the multiplication table, and the alphabet; more stuff hanging from lights and ceiling. I get a headache just walking into these classrooms. I'm not talking about having student work on the walls and all over the classroom, which is one of the best ways to celebrate and honor our students and their work. I'm talking about the teacher's stuff. (And there were certainly times when my own classroom was messy.) Maybe it's just me, but too much clutter in a room sets the wrong tone. The phrase people use for background clutter is "white noise." I don't believe that classrooms with a lot of white noise are conducive to productive and respectful learning and caring. The clutter seeps into our consciousness. There's a simple solution to this: Put out lots and lots of student work, but be organized and limited with your own things.

Keep Moving

Moving around while you teach can help with classroom management and student behavior in a number of ways. First, it puts you in closer contact with all of your students, not just the kids sitting or working at what is considered to be the front of the room. This tacitly tells your students that you care about all of them equally. Second, it gives a teacher what Jacob Kounin called *with-it-ness*, meaning the more you get around the room, the more you know what's going on around the room. If you're spending most of your time standing at the front of the classroom and José is reading a comic book in his lap, chances are you won't know it. The purpose of with-it-ness is not punitive; it's *preventive*. The more you get around the room, the more you can stop the little things from growing into big things. Just walking by

José should be enough to have him put away his comic book. Or you could just say his name. If those don't work, a pointed glance (or the "look") might do the trick. If that doesn't work, you could walk over by José and tap the comic book and whisper, "Away." But for you to choose to do any of these, you'd have to know that José has the comic book in the first place.

Another benefit of moving around is that you can help more kids and invite them into learning. When I'm observing in a classroom and the teacher is not moving around—and they're typically anchored at what is considered the front of the room—the students furthest away from the teacher are almost always completely withdrawn from what is happening. It's as if they aren't recognized as being in the room. You can see it in their body language. The simple solution to this is to walk around. I also suggest that teachers forget that there is a "front" of their classroom (the wall with the chalkboard). Teach as if there is no front.

First Do No Harm

This is the famous adage by Hippocrates, the Ancient Greek doctor. His point (which doctors today are still supposed to live by, part of the Hippocratic Oath) is that the first treatment should do the least amount of harm to the patient. If that doesn't work, then the doctor moves to the second least harmful, and so on, until he or she comes to more invasive treatments. The same idea can be applied to teaching. The scenario I gave with José reading the comic book can be an example. Some teachers would not walk by José and quietly have him put the comic book away. They would yell out his name from across the room, or walk over and snatch the book away, or give him a bad behavior "check," or give him a detention. Most situations don't need these reactions. A teacher first should do no harm. If José is reading a comic book when he's not supposed to, your purpose as a teacher is to simply refocus him to the task at hand. Remember, by far, most behavior problems in school are minor. Often it's how teachers react to them that can make them more serious (the same is true in parenting). One of the best—and harmless—ways to stop the little things like someone reading a comic book is to use humor. A little joke can so often get a kid right back on track, and it adds a little levity to the moment.

Does this mean that you can handle every disruption or misbehavior with a simple joke or a glance or a quick walk-by? Of course not. If José had his comic book out for the third time that day or even that week, I'd take it away. Remember that the first word here is *first*, which means you start at the least invasive reaction and progress from there. When I began teaching third, fourth, and fifth grade in Chicago, my students brought toys to school. I repeatedly tried the least invasive idea, letting my firsts do no harm, but it wasn't working. Some of my students continued to bring dolls or electronic "pets" or lanyard, and played with them at the wrong times, such as at class meetings. So I told my class that when they did this I was going to take away the toy and only give it back to a parent, and that's exactly what I did. It drastically reduced this problem.

Be a Model Learner and Be *Passionate!*

In Chapter 1 I discussed six ideas to think about. The first one was that if teachers make the work interesting, much of the discipline will take care of itself. One of the ways to make the work interesting is for the teacher to model being a passionate learner. Once again there is a huge difference between a teacher that teaches science and a teacher that is truly fascinated by science and devotes time outside of school to reading books and magazines and websites on science. Teachers that bring these habits of mind and passions with them into the classroom create an infectious learning environment. Along with that there are fewer behavior problems because more of the students are interested in what and how they are learning. This is probably my number one suggestion for teachers. Being a passionate lifelong learner might just be the most important quality a teacher can have, because these are the kinds of teachers that pass that passion on to their students. If we want our students to genuinely *care* about learning, then teachers need to care about learning, too, and by sharing that passion with our students we are helping them to be good.

Identify Students with Chronic Behavior Problems

As a teacher, if you hang out in teachers' lounges you'll hear teachers saying that if they could get rid of just one or two kids from their classroom their job would be infinitely easier. As I look back on my own classrooms over the years, I suppose this is true for myself as well; however, this is relative. As I wrote earlier, I had no serious behavior problems in my first school, but I did have a few kids who had worse behavior than others, and they did require more of my time.

The fact remains that many teachers do have students with chronic behavior problems, and I've seen in my own classrooms that often a handful of students (or just one) pulls other kids who would not act that way on their own to act poorly. Teachers can identify these students and work with them to improve their behavior. They can begin by making a list of the students with serious or chronic behavior problems. Try to keep the list very short; choose the kids that are creating the most difficulties and with whom you feel you can (and want to) work. Of course, helping these children is much more complex than it sounds, because as is often the case, kids with chronic behavior problems have other problems, such as low self-esteem, difficult home conditions, or problems with friends or peers, that contribute to or cause the problems in the first place.

The first thing I suggest when you identify a few of these students is to have some class free time. This may seem like an odd suggestion, but when the class has some free time to chat or play a board game or listen to some music, you start to see kids as they really are. Facades are torn away and kids are more relaxed to be themselves. While this is happening, watch what the kids on your list are doing. What they do is a value statement. It tells you something about each of them as a person, rather than as a "student." In my book, *A Democratic Classroom*, I wrote about a seventh-grade boy who was one my most difficult and frustrating students. He put forth little effort and was constantly disrupting the classroom. I bought a pile of board games and brought them into our classroom for free time and I was shocked to see that he was a passionate chess player. It changed how I saw him and interacted with him.

You can also learn about your students from activities you do in your classroom. Open discussions, journal writing, and activities with literature can help teachers get to know their students on a personal level. Teachers can also observe students during recess. Ask yourself: What makes this kid tick? What does he or she like to do? What are they interested in? What is life like for them outside of school? How do they see the world? How do they feel about themselves? What do they care about? Get to know your students as unique and complex people, try to see the world from their eyes, and take some time to develop good relationships. Admittedly, this is not easy, because kids with chronic behavior problems are so often the kids that frustrate teachers the most.

I also suggest spending some time with these kids one on one. Eat lunch with them, play a game of checkers during free time, chat with them as you walk the class to gym or art. And don't make these conversations about school. Use this informal talk as a chance for you to get to know the kids better and a chance for them to get to know *you* better. Talk about their hobbies (and your hobbies), what they did over the weekend (what you did over the weekend), their family (your family), what their favorite junk food is (what your favorite junk food is), and so on. A talk like this tears down the walls of "teacher" and "student" and becomes a friendly chat between two human beings. This can be especially important for kids with chronic behavior problems, as their relationships with teachers over the years have often been filled with animosity and conflict. (Actually, I'd suggest doing these same things with all of your students.)

Once you get to know a student with chronic behavior problems better there are some ideas you can try to help them improve. Depending on what you've learned about the student, one thing you can do is to get some help. You can talk to the student's parents (or meet with them with or without the student), the principal, the school social worker, the school psychologist, or a special education teacher. You can also talk to a teacher the student had in a previous year (or currently), but make sure you keep an open mind and remember that what you're hearing is their interpretation and opinion. Still, insight from past teachers, especially teachers that you respect or teachers that had a good relationship with the student, can help.

To specifically work on a student's behavior (once you've gotten to know them better) I suggest sitting down with them and having a private heart-to-heart talk, maybe even over lunch. Be honest, be direct, and be firm, but also be caring. Tell the student what you're feeling and how his or her behavior is so negatively affecting the class, your teaching, and their learning, but emphasize the necessity of respectful behavior in a classroom community. Exactly what you say will depend on what you've learned about the student. Make sure you give the student a lot of time to talk, and ask what you can do to help. But you still need to communicate that the behavior is unacceptable and that it cannot continue. Will this work? Sometimes yes, sometimes no; but you are building a better relationship with the student, and that can help.

If these ideas have no lasting benefits you can try other actions, including talking and possibly meeting with parents. Contacting parents is more complex than many believe. In my own experience with students with very bad behavior issues, I rarely saw any overall improvement in a student after I called a parent. If the parents could really help, I don't think I would have been having the problem in the first place. Typically if I contacted these parents, the student's behavior improved for a day or two and then they went right back to the lousy behavior. (Parents helped a lot more often with milder behavior problems, or poor behavior that is associated with social-emotional or medical issues.) And sometimes involving parents makes the situation worse. Still, there are times when the best course of action is to have a meeting with the parents and the student.

Sometimes a "contract" can be written at a meeting with parents and a student. (Or between just the teacher and the student.) Goals are agreed upon, some kind of reward is negotiated (something the student really values, like some extra time on the computer), the child writes up a simple contract, and everyone signs it. Coming from a strong democratic belief system I'm not a fan of behavior modification and actually hate the term. However, done in a simple, not labor-intensive, and humane way— and with very select students—it might be helpful.

There are times when just a simple verbal agreement can work even better, such as telling a student, "If you do well during project time today I'll let you go downstairs and read to a kindergartner during quiet reading time." Or even better: *Catch them being good* and then let them go and read to the kindergartners. Helping students with chronic and serious behavior problems by developing a good relationship, having some ongoing chats, giving some informal on-the-spot rewards and praise, helping them to succeed academically, and boosting their self-esteem all can help. This isn't easy and there are no magic solutions, but there are strategies teachers can try.

Structure Your Assignments

There are ways to structure an assignment that can help with student behavior. Much of this depends, of course, on the specific class and the individual students. However, I found it useful to create and pass out an assignment (or project) sheet at the start of a big project (Figure 3.1). When I first started to teach, my project sheets broke down each part of the assignment on a point system, but I eventually abandoned that because I did not want to emphasize quantitative assessment, but rather qualitative assessment with narrative and verbal responses. However, an assessment sheet with some form of point system can help (Figure 3.2).

Africa

An Exploration of Other Cultures

This class project will have us focus on the eastern coast of Africa. Each of you will do an individual project. You will probably have to focus on a specific geographic location for your project, and possibly even an area within a single country. Some of the countries that you may want to learn about include: Kenya, Somalia, Ethiopia, Madagascar, etc. Specifically what you want to research is up to you, but your topic must be approved. As we discussed in class, some of the sub-topics you can choose to explore include: religion, art, architecture, myths and stories, daily life, history, social and/or economic problems, government, geography, etc. Exactly what you choose to research, as well as what your final product will be (write and illustrate a children's picture book, a brochure, an annotated timeline, etc.) will be detailed in your project plan. Remember, your project plan must be fully approved before your begin your work.

There are some requirements for your project:

- All writing must be revised, self-edited, and teacher edited, with all final copies typed.
- You need to include at least one visual (a map, pictures, etc.)
- You need to maintain and turn in a complete list of resources used.
- Complete a self-evaluation once your project is finished.

Important Dates

Project Plan Due: Monday, November 7

Start Research: Wednesday, November 9

Research Check: Monday, November 21

End Research/Start Final Project: Friday, December 2

Project Due/Presentation: Tuesday, December 20

FIGURE 3.1

American Revolution Board Game Project

<u>Assessment Sheet</u>

Name _____ Date _____

Other Group Members _____

You will be assessed (and you will self-assess) primarily on your overall **effort, thoughtfulness,** and **quality** for each part of the project.

Do your best work!

		Self- Assessment	Teacher Assessment
Research Notes	(20 points)	_____	_____
Board Game	(40 points)	_____	_____
Written Game Instructions (15 points)		_____	_____
Group Membership & Participation (25 points)		_____	_____
Total Points	(100)	_____	_____

Narrative Self-Assessment (continue on back). Answer three questions: 1) Why did you give yourself the points (and total points) above? 2) What are you most proud of in this project? 3) If you were to do this project again, what would you do differently?

FIGURE 3.2

How can sheets like these help with behavior? First, right from the beginning of an assignment kids have a schedule, which helps them to focus and remain "on task." Knowing that their research notes are due on a specific date and their final "product" is due on another date helps kids maintain a good work ethic. Second, sheets such as these hold students accountable for completing the expected work and encourages them to do their best work. When I passed out the sheet shown in Figure 3.1 my students knew right from the start that I was going to check their work on a specific date. Teaching is messy and unpredictable, so that date can change, but the kids still know that they're responsible for turning in a specific piece of work at a given time. Once again I have a bigger purpose here. The sheet is really to help my students learn about scheduling and responsibility.

Use Self-Assessment

Self-assessment may be the best form of assessment. Assessing ourselves throughout our lives is one of the finest qualities we can have. It is the regular reflection and judgment of ourselves. People who self-assess ask themselves questions such as, Am I being a good father or mother? How am I spending my time? Do I watch too much television? Do I read enough? How am I treating others? Am I taking care of my body? Am I doing enough to help the environment? Am I doing a good job painting the family room? Is the report I prepared for work high enough quality? At their best these questions are about more than just assessment, they are about *improvement* and *doing our best*. And for many people, self-assessment is a moral guide. They check their daily actions against their moral "code" of what is right and wrong, what is good and bad.

Helping kids make self-assessment a regular part of their school experience can have powerful results. I regularly used different forms of self-assessment. At times I'd have my students write a narrative self-assessment in their journals. I'd also have them prepare a more formal narrative self-assessment as part of their report card each quarter by having them write about the two things in school they're most proud of and the two things in school they need to improve on the most (including academics and behavior). When I had to complete a traditional report card for my students with letter grades and behavior checkmarks (as opposed to a narrative report card with no grades), I first photocopied a blank report card and had each student fill out their own report card for grades and behavior. I told my students that if they took their self-assessments seriously, I would, too, in determining their grades. I rarely had a student inflate a grade. When treated with respect and honesty, kids are honest about their work and behavior, and they're more accepting of constructive criticism.

I also made self-assessment a topic of frequent class discussions. It's important for this to happen when kids have had both bad and good behavior. Far too often teachers only talk with kids about their behavior when it's been poor. Talking with kids, and speaking honestly about your proud feelings when they've been great, is just as important. Self-assessment during discussions can be especially beneficial. For example, after a particularly good (or bad) writing workshop, I might have the class sit in a circle on the rug and take a little time to process their behavior and the work they did. I might begin by saying, "Okay, how do you think we did as a class during writing workshop today?" Or I could simplify this by asking, "I want five kids to rate how we did during writing workshop today. Zero through ten, with ten being an out-of-this-world-phenomenal-writing-workshop." After the students rated or talked about how they did, I always gave my opinion and did not hesitate to be honest. If they were phenomenal, I told them so; if they were terrible, I told them that, too; and if it was mixed, I would explain my opinion, sometimes naming kids who were great and kids who were disruptive. My purpose here was not to punish or lecture, but to talk and discuss and educate.

Self-assessment can also be used for students' work. For example, Figures 3.2 and 3.3 are two different self-assessment sheets that could be used for a project (in this case, on the American Revolution). From time to time I would also have my students complete a classroom community self-assessment (Figure 3.4). When my students worked on projects in groups, I sometimes had them complete a self-assessment (Figure 3.5).

Be Prepared

Not being prepared gives kids "downtime," and downtime gives them chances to get into trouble. While some downtime can be great (use it for some free time or to do a quick, on-the-spot activity or game), too much of it can influence poor behavior. The solution here is simple: Try your best to be prepared.

American Revolution Project Evaluation Sheet

Name _____ Date _____

Student Self-Evaluation

1. Mid-research grade (will be done on Friday, February 16):
   ✓+   ✓   ✓–

2. What am I most proud of on this project?

3. If someone starting this project now came to me for help, what advice would I give them?

4. How would I rate my overall effort on this project?

Low   1   2   3   4   5   6   7   8   9   10   High

5. The final grade I would give myself is: ✓+   ✓   ✓–

Teacher Evaluation

1. Mid-research grade (Friday, February 16):   ✓+   ✓   ✓–

2. Overall effort:

Low   1   2   3   4   5   6   7   8   9   10   High

3. Final Grade: ✓+   ✓   ✓–

My Narrative Comments (written on the back of this sheet):

FIGURE 3.3

Community & Individual Self-Evaluation

Name _____ Date _____

1. What does community mean to you?

2. In what ways is our classroom working great as a community?

3. In what ways is our classroom not working well as a community?

4. Rate how you are doing to make our classroom community work great:

Very Poor   1   2   3   4   5   6   7   8   9   10   Excellent

5. What two goals will make you a better community member?

6. What changes would you suggest to improve our classroom community? (Write your ideas on the back of this sheet.)

FIGURE 3.4

Social Issue Survey Project

Group Self-Evaluation

Name _____ Survey Topic _____ Date _____

Other Group Members _____

(After you, I will offer my grade and comments on the identical sheet and return it.)

1. Describe how well the group worked together. What worked well and what didn't?

2 Rate how well the grouped worked together:

Very Poorly   1   2   3   4   5   6   7   8   9   10   Great

3. Rate how well you worked as a group member:

Very Poorly   1   2   3   4   5   6   7   8   9   10   Great

4. Grade yourself on this overall project: 3+   3   3–

5. What contributions did you make to your group?

6. If a group about to start this project came to you for help, what advice would you give them? (Write your ideas on the back of this sheet.)

FIGURE 3.5

Keep in Mind Cultural Influences
on Behavior and Learning

Our culture has a powerful affect on our reality, on how we see the world and the "rules" we live by. By *culture* I am referring to more than just ethnicity and race, but also economic culture, gender, culture of one's neighborhood and geographic region, as well as the unique culture of a family system and home life. This last point is important because you can have a class that's entirely Latino, and while many of them (or perhaps all) will share some common ethnic culture, each of the kids comes from his or her own family culture, which is different.

Cultural experience has a powerful influence on a person's behavior. Lisa Delpit (1988) has had much to say on this issue. She points out how many white middle-class teachers unknowingly bring their white middle-class reality with them into their classrooms. This reality, Delpit argues, is profoundly different from the reality of most lower-income children, and specifically she writes of African American kids. She offers the following example:

> Middle-class parents are likely to give the directive to a child to take his bath as, "Isn't it time for your bath?" Even though the utterance is couched as a question, both the child and adult understand it as a directive. The child may respond with, "Aw, Mom, can't I wait until . . . ," but whether or not negotiation is attempted, both conversants understand the intent of the utterance.
>
> By contrast, a Black mother, in whose house I was recently a guest, said to her eight-year-old son, "Boy, get your rusty behind in that bathtub." Now I happen to know that this woman loves her son as much as any mother, but she would never have posed the directive to her son to take a bath in the form of a question. Were she to ask, "Would you like to take your bath now?" she would not have been issuing a directive but offering a true alternative. Consequently, as Heath suggests, upon entering school the child from such a family may not understand the indirect statement of the teacher as a direct command. (p. 289)

Delpit's point resonated with me when I started to teach in a Chicago public school. Coming from a suburban school with affluent students, as well as my own suburban upbringing, I brought my white upper-middle-class assumptions into my classroom and expected my students to follow right along. The result of not being cognizant of their own cultural realities, and the cultural realities of their students, can mean teachers implement a progressive teaching methodology like whole language or project-based learning as if their students share and understand the language, meanings, and "rules" from that way of life. This can further result in poor student behavior because the kids may be looking for explicit directives from a clear authority figure, and what they have is a teacher that expects them to work in a more self-directed, "Isn't it time to take your bath?" manner. This can perpetuate bad behavior and academic failure in school. (My student Laura implies this point about her own teaching in Chapter 1.)

I don't believe this means that teachers should change their philosophy about teaching low-income and/or culturally diverse children and become more traditional, or that they should tell (or yell at) their kids to move their "rusty behinds." But they must be mindful of their students' cultural realities, and be open to *adjusting* their teaching when necessary, such as adding more structure or being more direct. Teachers *can* be more direct *without* being autocratic, while still being *democratic*. Teachers can also help kids understand more passive directives. If children don't know how (and why) to live in a self-directed manner, part of the job of teaching in a democratic classroom is to teach them this knowledge. (This is exactly what Laura does with her students.)

Urban children, many of whom are African American and Hispanic, and are either poor or the "working poor," are the victims of terrible educational stereotypes. Many people (the media, politicians, society at large, some educators) assume that all "urban" students don't want to learn, can't learn, misbehave, and are lazy. Many teachers avoid progressive teaching practices with these kids because they assume their students will run wild. My experiences in both teaching in urban schools and spending much time in urban classrooms have shown me that this is not the case. By far, most kids in urban classrooms want to learn, want to do well in school, and are good. Many children in urban and impoverished schools lack the skills and the basic life knowledge to complete their work with high quality, but they do come to school to learn and they are capable of great success in progressive classrooms with the proper support, guidance, and expectations.

Culture also has a profound influence on learning. We are all sociocultural beings, meaning we all live and develop and learn in cultural contexts—both in school and out. Culture is not only part of the *content* we learn in these contexts, but also equally part of the learning *process*.

This cultural knowledge forms our everyday realities. This is Lisa Delpit's point when she argues that children from different cultural and economic contexts come to school with different knowledge, rules, and expectations about authority in school. These realities frame how children will act and behave inside their classrooms, and what they will learn.

Given these crucial roles of culture on our learning, it is recommended that teachers strive to create *culturally relevant* classrooms (Brown, 2002; Ladson-Billings, 1994). Some of the characteristics of culturally relevant teaching are the following:

- a belief that all children can learn and succeed

- situating curriculum (content, knowledge, skills, etc.) in the lives and cultures of the students, and striving to help students make connections between the knowledge and their lives

- teachers that get to know their students' lives, interests, and cultures

- using "materials and resources that reflect students' cultural values, history, and beliefs" (Brown, p. 113)

- a respect for different learning styles and "intelligences" (Gardner, 1983)

- recognition of a possible dissonance between a teacher's cultural realities and his or her students' cultural realities

- teachers who value and use the existing knowledge children bring with them into their classrooms

- recognition that much of the learning is done in groups

- a belief that knowledge is taught critically to promote critical literacy

One example of culturally relevant teaching is my suggestion for teachers to use much children's literature that is situated in their students' cultures. A second example is offered by Ladson-Billings of a fifth-grade teacher teaching the U.S. Constitution to African American students. She writes, "[The teacher] might begin with a discussion of the bylaws and articles of incorporation that were used to organize a local church or African American civic association" (p. 18). Doing this not only situates some of the concepts of the Constitution (such as "written rules") within many of the students' existing schema, but also, as Ladson-Billings points out, it also teaches that "their own people are institution-builders."

Pay Attention to the Kids

Good teachers focus on multiple things while they teach. They focus on their teaching, on the content, on the clock, and especially on their students. It's important for teachers to constantly read their students as they teach. Teachers can learn a great deal from studying the atmosphere of their class and the mindset and body language of their students. A lot of students slumping in their seats says something. So does a normally verbal and active class becoming very quiet. A class of students whose minds and bodies and mouths are racing a mile a minute says something, too. Consider some of the possible variables affecting your students' attitudes, focus, and energy, such as the kids' private lives, as well as the life of the community and neighborhood. As we all know, things happen to people outside of school that have a tremendous influence on their attitudes and behavior in school. I had a fourth-grade girl in my class a few years ago whose parents suddenly split up. Not surprisingly it consumed every minute of her day. A mature and respectful and hard-working kid was now belligerent and doing little schoolwork. The same thing happens to kids when there is upheaval in their social lives, or when something tragic happens in the community or the school. When I was a kid and I was going through a difficult time with peer pressure, that's what consumed my mind. I could not care less about what I was supposed to learn.

Another major influence on children's attitudes is what they're being made to do by the teacher. Watch kids' faces as a teacher lectures for thirty, forty, fifty minutes, and you will usually see a clear message. If a teacher does have to give a long lecture or demonstration, I suggest taking a break for a few minutes and letting the kids stretch. As teachers work they need to watch their teaching from the perspectives of their students. If that perspective is saying, "I'm bored and tired, it's a good time to take a break."

The kind of day it is outside—which comes into the room from the windows—can influence the day you have inside the classroom. A dark and gloomy day can bring down the entire class, causing them to drag. A beautiful sunny day (especially in the spring after a long winter) can do the opposite, launching kids to life and bringing out their energy from winter hibernation. As teachers we need to take these issues into account and understand that our students are human just like us. If you think the day (or something else) is distracting the kids, maybe the best thing to do is to forget about your plans and do something entirely different. We need to stop blaming kids every time they have a bad day. Adults have bad days, too (including teachers). Sometimes we have obligations or time constraints and we need to forge ahead and do the best we can, but other times we should toss aside those lesson plans and "objectives" and chase the wind.

Ignore Some Behavior

One good way to stop poor behavior is to ignore it. Sometimes kids do things just to get attention. Teachers can choose not to give it to them. Sometimes this works and sometimes it doesn't, but there are times when it may be worth a try.

Think about Classroom Rules

In the last chapter I wrote briefly on classroom rules. I'm going to elaborate on that here. Most classrooms during the first week of school talk about (or lecture about) some kind of classroom rules and perhaps post them on the wall. There's nothing wrong with having rules; I suppose rules in a classroom are like laws in a society. But there are different ways of thinking about rules that could open up some new possibilities. One way is the idea I wrote about in Chapter 2, which is considering having classroom *values* instead of or in addition to rules. Here are some other ideas to consider when thinking about classroom rules:

- If you have written rules, keep them simple. I suggest no more than five written rules. Too many rules, and they get lost in the crowd.

- Let the kids write the five written rules, or at least have a say in what they are. Once you give kids voice, you need to honor that voice. This means you'll probably have to pare down what you and the class come up with into a workable short list of rules. At the very least, a teacher can *discuss* class rules rather than dictate rules.

- Rules don't need to be written in stone. They can be changed.

- During my first years of teaching we had one classroom rule on a large sign: OUR ONE RULE: MUTUAL RESPECT. We talked about this rule a lot.

- You don't have to have written rules. You can *talk* about rules, expectations, and good habits of mind; they don't *have* to be written and posted.

- Classroom rules can be in other forms. The class can write a Classroom Constitution and/or a Students' (and teacher's) Bill of Rights. (See Brodhagen, 1995, and Fleming, 1996, for examples of classes writing a constitution.)

- Classroom rules can have listed consequences, but I wouldn't recommend it. Once you have consequences listed in very concrete ink, you'll feel obliged to stick with them (and get angry when you don't), which puts teachers at a disadvantage. As I explain in the following section, having rigid consequences can be problematic, and teachers, like parents, bend their own rules.

- Most rules are intended for the students, but teachers need to follow them as well. A teacher could also consider writing, or having the kids write, a set of rules for the *teacher* to follow. Here's an example: "Mr. Wolk will always strive to make our learning relevant." If you're going to post rules, you might want to have two sets of rules side-by-side, one for the kids and one for you. Or at the very least, label the class rules as applying to the students and the teacher, perhaps as "classroom community rules."

- A teacher can ignore the idea of having rules at the start of the year, and instead, discuss or write rules as they become necessary. Beginning the year with the rule, "All students must raise their hand to speak," assumes from the start that at least some of the kids won't do this. That might not be the case, which means you don't need that rule.

- The purpose of rules should not be to hold kids to a set of ironclad laws and punish them when they break one. Classroom management from a democratic perspective sees classroom rules as an ongoing opportunity to *teach kids* about issues of character, behavior, responsibility, social justice, and the common good. Rather than being punitive or even preventive, rules can (and should) be *educative*.

Being Just Is More Important Than Being Consistent

Some teachers believe that when it comes to student behavior and consequences, they need to be consistent. The reasoning goes like this: If teachers aren't consistent with responses to behavior issues, then their students won't take their rules or expectations seriously. But I think it's more important for a teacher to be *just* (or fair) than to be consistent. Since all kids are different and all situations are unique, teachers need to respond to each situation in its context. Take, for example, the well-behaved fourth-grade girl I wrote about whose parents suddenly split up (I'll call her Angela), and another fourth-grade girl who chronically disrupts the classroom (I'll call her Jenny). If both were to disrupt the classroom, in separate situations, by getting into a loud shouting and pushing match with another student, should I respond the same way for both kids? Angela virtually never gets into trouble, and Jenny gets into a lot of trouble. I know Angela is acting the way she is because of what's happening in her family. (The same could be true for Jenny, or there could be another personal issue I don't know about. I can't make assumptions, but I have to do the best that I can.) As a teacher I feel that I must take into account more than simply what the girls are doing. I need to look at the situation holistically and make my decisions. Sometimes that means I may give only one of the girls a consequence, or I may give them different consequences, or I may given neither of them consequences. That, to me, is being just.

I can still have rules or expectations. I'm not going to ignore or condone the behavior of Angela, and I'm not going to be harder on Jenny because of her past behavior. I'm going to communicate to both that what they are doing is wrong. But exactly what I say and what I do may differ, depending on the situation. Even knowing about Angela's home situation I may still respond the same way. It depends on the immediate context, and that has many variables that I need to consider. (And I've made mistakes, being both too lenient and too hard.) There's also nothing wrong with waiting to decide how you're going to handle a situation. Sometimes the best thing for a teacher to do is to take some time, and maybe even talk to the kids involved later, after they (and you) have had some time to think.

Don't Use Schoolwork as Punishment

It has become accepted practice in so many schools to make students do extra schoolwork as punishment. The most common form of this is to make kids write something, such as "I will not talk in class," one hundred times, a "reflective" essay, dictionary definitions, or a letter home to a parent. Sadly, this doesn't stop with writing. Students get extra math problems, extra reading, and extra textbook assignments, all in the name of punishing bad behavior.

The only lesson this teaches children is to hate writing (or math or reading or whatever) and to equate learning and schoolwork with punishment and being bad. If a teacher is committed to nurturing a love of lifelong learning, teaching students that writing or reading or math is something you do more of for punishment works *against* that idea. Overall, I think teachers would be better off rewarding good behavior than punishing bad behavior (more on this shortly). If you do feel the need to punish, I suggest taking away a privilege, such as recess or free time, which I have done.

There are limited times when writing can be used with behavior issues, such as having two (or more) kids write their version of what happened surrounding an incident. But I don't view that as punishment, and it's important to stress that to the students. The reasoning is for kids to use writing for two of its primary purposes: to help us reflect and to help us communicate. Writing on behavior can also be done as a part of class journal writing, and that again isn't for punishment, but for thinking and learning and sharing. So, writing can be used to help kids learn about behavior, character, and goodness, but within the context of being educational, not punitive.

Emphasize Good Behavior (and Limit Rewards)

While rewards should be used over punishment, I don't believe giving rewards in school should be done that much, if at all. Rewards can be used with individual students or a class with chronic behavior problems, but they should always be seen as a means to an end—that is, a way to help kids learn to be good *without* rewards—rather than an end in itself. Some teachers use reward systems to help their whole class have good behavior. An example is putting marbles in a jar when the students are good and removing marbles when the students are bad. (When the jar is filled they have a class party or watch a movie or something.) I've never done this, and I wouldn't want to tell teachers not to do it, but I would encourage teachers to try to *reframe* (see Chapter 1) behavior problems before they try a reward system. For example, teachers can consider my point of "making the work interesting and the discipline will take care of itself" by examining what they're making their students do. Or we can examine our daily schedules and consider changes, or we can change the seating arrangement, or have a class meeting and talk with the kids about the behavior.

I agree with Alfie Kohn (1993) who strongly argues that rewarding students is damaging. When teachers do this they are paying kids to behave or do certain work. This does little to help kids to be good because it is important, enjoyable, and the morally correct way to act. Rewarding or paying kids to do things reduces questions of human behavior to a business transaction. Rather than simply rewarding students for doing the right thing, we should be helping them to explore issues of character. Then they will do the right thing because it's *right*. Kids should learn and read not because they get a slice of pizza or a smiley-face sticker, but because learning and reading are great. Does this take more time? Absolutely. But the purpose should be to help shape an entire person over the long term, rather than to "manage" a specific behavior for the moment.

There are simpler ways of emphasizing good behavior that have nothing to do with rewards. Imagine you're picking up your students from art class and they're all lined up at the door, but they're noisy and rambunctious, and a cacophony of voices is everywhere. But there are some kids who aren't doing that; they're standing in line quietly waiting to go back to your classroom. Instead of talking to the noisy kids and trying to get them to quiet down, a teacher can talk to the quiet kids. A few comments such as, "Great job in line, Jessica," or "Thanks for being ready to go, Pedro," can help get the noisy kids to quiet down. As the noisy kids settle down, you can start saying something positive to them.

Have Kids Sit in Front of You as a Group

When I started teaching in Chicago I struggled with having my students stay focused when I'd read aloud a novel or a picture book or when I was doing a mini-lesson. At first I would do these with my students sitting at their desks or tables, and I was either walking around the room (reading aloud) or at the board or an overhead projector (for most mini-lessons). I made a very simple change that helped tremendously: I had the class sit in front of me on the rug.

When kids get older many teachers stop having them sit on a rug or come together as an entire class. Rarely do I see older students (fifth grade and up) sitting on the floor before their teacher as he or she reads aloud. They're always at their desks. Having students sit on the floor for reading aloud or mini-lessons worked so well that I would suggest it for any class in any school at any grade. For our read aloud, not only did the kids stay focused a lot more when they sat before me, but they enjoyed the book infinitely more because they were literally into the story in a physical sense; they were so close to me. And it was easier for me to pull the kids into the story dramatically because we were so close.

When kids are at their desks it's too easy for their minds to wander, even during a mini-lesson (which typically lasts no longer than fifteen minutes). Rather than having the students scattered around the room as I explained how to take research notes or how to use a dictionary, I had them right in front of me on our large rug, and sometimes I had them take notes in their journals. I especially like Nancie Atwell's (1998) idea of using a pad of chart paper on an easel for mini-lessons (or you could use a small dry erase board on an easel), while all of the kids sit before her on the floor.

Try Hard Not to Yell

Like it or not, teachers are moral models to their students (Fenstermacher, 1990; Hansen, 1992). Everything teachers do implicitly says to children, this is the way you should act. As I wrote earlier, everything a teacher does in the classroom is a value statement. From the content we teach, to our teaching methods, to the room arrangement, to our relationship with our students, to what we put on our walls—it's all saying, "This is what I value." Perhaps the most powerful way to help kids be good is for their teachers to be good. This means that teachers should try their hardest not to yell at their students.

Yelling, to me, is an act of violence. There were times (gladly not many) that I yelled at my students. I was always mad at myself afterward for doing it, for not being a better person and staying calm. And when I did yell, I later apologized to my students and told them that I was wrong. Teaching is one of the most human and emotional jobs one can have, and that means there will be times when our frustration will get the best of us. Kids can be quite good at pushing teachers' buttons, so it's important for us to be in tune with our buttons and cognizant of what can set them off. I remember a few times when I walked away from a student before I became angry with him or her. Some teachers don't like to admit they get angry or frustrated with a student or a class, so we must end this romance and admit that we are human beings.

This does not mean it's wrong for teachers to raise their voices. People have told me that I have a good "teacher's voice," and they mean that I use inflections and tones in my voice to my advantage. Raising or projecting or focusing your voice is different from yelling. Yelling usually has anger behind it; projecting or directing your voice doesn't.

Assume Goodness

Too often adults assume kids are going to be bad. I consider this a form of prejudice against young people. My experiences with kids have taught me that, more often than not, kids can make the right choices and be good. Teachers need to begin with goodness; they need to walk into their classrooms with the assumption that their students are good people and are capable of making good decisions. This does not excuse bad behavior and it does not require teachers to relinquish their authority or their guidance. But there is a huge difference between a teacher that begins with the assumption that children are lazy, will go out of their way to be bad, and are incapable of making a good decision, and a teacher that begins with the assumption that kids want to work hard, learn, and be good. We need to have faith and trust in kids. We need to believe that they have goodness.

Teaching *for* Goodness

*We must recognize that the goal of education is not
mastery of knowledge, but the mastery of self
through knowledge—a different thing altogether.*
— David Orr (1995)

The purpose of this chapter is to offer strategies, ideas, and methods on how teachers can teach kids to be good, or at least to think about being good and what that means to them. Obviously, this is not about standing at the front of the class and lecturing on the virtues of goodness. It is about giving kids regular opportunities to examine self and community and life, and to reflect on and struggle with difficult and complex questions and issues regarding our behavior, actions, and character, both individually and collectively. Some of these activities are specifically done for the purpose of having kids examine their value systems, character, moral identities, and goodness. Most of these ideas, however, should be part of a larger curricular purpose, such as a project on the rainforest or the American Civil War or simply a class discussion on something in the news. While these topics or lessons are not done expressly to help kids be good, all of them can incorporate issues of goodness within the topics. I believe that it is possible to integrate goodness, character, social justice, values, morality and ethics, behavior, and self-discipline into every school subject and virtually any curricular topic. And at its best this teaching is integrated throughout each day.

Many of the teaching ideas here involve open talk and discussion. This is one of the primary ways children and adults can explore issues of behavior and character: by talking about them. Letting children talk in school is usually considered being *bad*, not being good. But allowing kids to talk—that is, helping them and teaching them to engage in discussion on thoughtful and important and difficult issues and ideas—is not only central to being human and a biologically social animal, but is also central to democracy and community. Good, or "strong" democracy (Barber, 1985) involves people engaging in this regular discourse. Consider some of the benefits of having students engage in discussion:

- thinking about and shaping their own ideas, opinions, and experiences about a topic—they shape their selves

- making connections between the topics and their lives

- hearing and considering other perspectives (including the teacher's)

- learning the content under discussion

- learning the value of discourse and its role in a democratic society

- creating new knowledge, as opposed to simply memorizing someone else's predetermined knowledge

- getting ideas and taking actions that can make the world a better place (Preskill, 1997)

Far from being bad, having kids regularly participate in good talk and discussion is being very, very good.

Class Meetings

Class meetings are about giving children regular opportunities to talk. They are a "formal" time to have kids engage in real discussion about important issues (Glasser, 1969). These ideas and topics can come from a variety of sources: the teacher; the kids' lives; newspapers and magazines; pop culture; happenings and problems in the classroom, the school, and the neighborhood; the school curriculum; and the media. Class meetings allow kids to talk and debate about being good. Not all class meetings are about topics having to do with goodness. In fact, the topic of "being good" is rarely the specific topic being discussed. More often issues of goodness and character are embedded in a "larger" topic under discussion. Here are ten topics that I've discussed with my students at class meetings that involve issues of goodness:

- ethnic slurs

- violence

- classroom and school behavior problems

- natural disasters (and aid from countries)

- video games

- war

- prejudice (racism, sexism, stereotyping, xenophobia, classism, homophobia)

- television and movies

- the death penalty

- using and abusing the classroom supplies

One of the best uses of class meetings is to discuss problems you're having in the classroom community, including behavior problems. Often when kids are "bad," students hear a lecture or write for punishment, and parents are called, notes are sent home, or they're sent to the principal. This does not include giving the students time to talk about the problem, reflect on it, hear other perspectives (especially from other kids), and grow from it. Talking about our problems and mistakes outside of school is one of the most powerful ways of understanding our actions and improving ourselves. Outside of school—in the "real world"—adults (and kids) talk about their problems all of the time. We talk to friends, family members, clergy, therapists and counselors, and co-workers. As we talk about our dilemmas we make sense of them; we see other perspectives, get new ideas, and try to improve and solve. That's the same idea for class meetings, which are just as powerful with first graders as they are with middle school and high school kids. Giving students regular opportunities to talk allows them—actually *encourages* them—to consciously understand who they are and create who they want to be, and that's being good.

In my classrooms I had two different kinds of class meetings. We started each day with a "morning meeting," and we ended each day with a "class meeting." For both meetings we all sat in a circle on our large rug. (When I taught in a Chicago public school with a shorter school day I combined both meetings into a longer morning meeting. If I were to teach now I would only have this one longer class meeting in the morning.) Our morning meetings were about twenty-five minutes long. As soon as my students entered the room they sat on the rug. I sat with them and brought two newspapers, the *New York Times* and *Chicago Tribune*. After a few minutes of business (attendance, lunch count, etc.) we talked about one of two topics: news in our lives or news from the world. Both of these have endless issues of goodness to talk about. For example, if a student (or a teacher) has a relative who is ill or who has died, this can lead to a discussion about caring and empathy, and that's being good. The same can come from a discussion about an earthquake in Mexico, poverty in India, or a local fire with a heroic firefighter, all of which can come from the newspaper.

Class meetings at the end of the day had a different purpose. They were primarily about problem solving. At these meetings we talked about "larger" issues: war, poverty, racism, sexism, pollution, problems with government and citizenship, successes and failures of social justice, and dilemmas in our own classroom. Many of these topics came from the kids; I wanted them to know that they had an opportunity on most days to talk about something that was important to them, but I also framed the purpose of class meetings at the beginning of the year. For all of our meetings my role as the facilitator was crucial. I encouraged my students to talk, helped them make connections, taught them how to listen, and redirected the conversation. I did not shy away from offering my own perspectives on a topic. That's my job: to help my students think in new ways and create new knowledge and understanding. And I usually pulled issues of goodness out of the topics being discussed. I wanted to specifically help my students look at these everyday issues through a lens of morality, character, social justice, and goodness. Not in every class meeting, but certainly in many if them, if they didn't bring up these dimensions, then I did.

Journal Writing

The purposes of using journals with children are the same as when adults write in journals and diaries: to write to think about and shape ideas, help us to understand and create ourselves, and ponder life. Writing allows us to form our identities. Peter Elbow (1973) wrote, "Writing is a way to end up thinking something you couldn't have started out thinking" (p. 15). Writing is a creation process; we don't first figure out what to write and then put words on paper. Rather we create and make sense as we write, as a product of the experience. Plus, if we share our journal writing with each other (such as I did with my students), our identity development becomes a social act and we learn from each other.

There are an infinite number of ways to use journals in a classroom to have students explore being good. Perhaps the simplest way is for teachers to give students prompts for them to write about. Teachers need to take these prompts seriously. Often they're simplistic or cute when they can be deeply intellectual, even with younger kids. Here are ten journal prompts that can encourage kids to think about being good:

1. Write about a time you did something good and/or bad.
2. Write about how you think adults misunderstand kids.
3. Write about someone (living or dead) that is/was a good person and what made him or her a good person.
4. Write about one social injustice that you have a strong opinion about. What is it? Why is it important to you? What can we do to stop it? (Or write about a specific injustice, such as the pay inequity between men and women: Why does it exist? Does it connect to you in any way? What can we do to end it?)
5. What do you value? Write about two things, characteristics, or ideas that you value and why you value them.
6. Write about a time when someone hurt your feelings or a time when you hurt someone else's feelings.

7. What needs to be improved in our community? How can we, individually and collectively, make our neighborhood a better place?
8. Is it okay to make and market violent video games? Why or why not?
9. Should we have gun control? Why or why not?
10. What is a good citizen?

Students can also write about specific events, such as a local tragedy. If a student was picked-on or teased during recess, he or she can write about that in the journal. If someone in the school or the community does something good, he or she can write on that. Thoughtful topics to write about are all around us, because issues of being good are all around us. (We need to be careful not to drown our students with these issues; there is much more to write about in life than behavior and character.)

Students can also do freewriting in their journals. This is when they are free to write about anything they wish. I had my students do freewriting once a week. (The one or two other journal writings each week were on specific topics.) One of the great benefits of freewriting is that children are "naturally" writing about ideas and experiences that are meaningful and relevant, because their writings are coming from them.

As teachers, however, we need to be aware that we are all social and cultural beings, meaning we are all part of larger sociocultural and sociopolitical contexts. So what we write, even "naturally," is not really as "free" as it appears. If a student chooses to write a story about space aliens coming to earth and waging war, he did that for a reason. While he may have "freely" chosen that topic, we need to ask *why* he chose that topic in the first place, or why the space aliens waged war instead of coming to earth to plant flowers. Inside our students' writings are powerful social, cultural, and political constructs, and as teachers we need to *exploit* these "natural" opportunities to help our students interrogate them. If a student writes about student cliques on the playground during recess, imbedded in that text are issues of power (and perhaps gender and culture) that we can explore with our students. What so often seems routine and every day are socially and politically constructed realities. Teachers can write back to their students in their journals (or just talk with them), nudging them to excavate those constructs and examine them from different perspectives. Randy Bomer (1999) and John Gaughan (1999) have written provocatively that our students' writings are full of opportunities for teachers to help kids explore the complex political and social layers of their everyday lives.

When my students wrote in their journals I wrote in my own journal. One year I did a little action research. I wanted to see if my students would write more in their journals if I wrote more in my journal and shared it with the class. That's exactly what happened. If we wrote in our journals for fifteen or twenty minutes and I filled two or three pages, some of my students did the same. My students started to write more because I wrote more. My students took their journal writing seriously because I took my journal writing seriously and because much of what we were writing about were important issues. The words and ideas that I put down on the pages of my journal and shared with my students were real and passionate, and children appreciate passion.

Using the Newspaper

Daily newspapers are filled with issues, questions, and controversies of goodness. As I wrote before, I brought the *New York Times* and *Chicago Tribune* to my classroom every day. I wanted newspapers to be a part of our classroom culture; they helped make our room intellectual and informed. I kept newspapers in our classroom library and invited my students to read them. I wanted to celebrate newspapers and help my students to understand that reading a newspaper, which can keep us informed and promote critical literacy and good citizenship, is being good.

Newspapers are perfect to use with journals. Borrowing an idea from Vikki Proctor and Ken Kantor (1996), I did "social issue journal writing" regularly with my students (Wolk, 1998). I copied a newspaper article, editorial cartoon, comic, editorial, or an op-ed article, passed out copies to the class, had them read it, and then read it aloud. After we wrote in our journals in response to the articles, we sat on our rug to share our thoughts. (First those that wanted to read shared what they wrote and then I opened it up for discussion.) The emphasis of our discussions was not just about the students understanding what they read, but was deeply constructivist: I wanted to help them make sense of what the article meant to each of them, help them to connect it to their lives and existing knowledge, encourage them to share these personal meanings and opinions, and help them listen to the thoughts of others. These discussions were about children as knowledge creators, and they were some of the best experiences I've had with kids. Exploring these everyday events with children can help them to:

- shape their behavior, character, and self

- develop empathy and compassion

- learn about the content in the story (government, geography, economics, art, healthcare, the business and ethics of sports, culture—the list is endless)

- think for themselves on complex issues

- care about important ideas

- read the newspaper and be informed citizens

- participate in civic matters and to understand that how we act—our behavior—is a crucial element in a democratic society

- understand and act for social justice

Using newspapers (and the "news") need not be limited to older students. Teachers of children in every grade can make these an important part of their classrooms. A great teacher I know, Amy Rome, created a sheet for her first graders tos use for "current events," which she then used to facilitate class discussions (see Figure 4.1).

Let's take an actual paper and look inside. We'll look at the *New York Times* for Friday, February 9, 2001. First I'll list every article that could be used to help students explore behavior, character, social justice, and goodness. After that, I'll pick three articles and look at them in more detail.

Section A (Main News)

Bush Tax Plan Sent to Congress, Starting the Jostling for Position
Milosevic Facing Arrest by Serbs for a Local Trial
Cosmetic Saves a Cure for Sleeping Sickness
Ex-Wife of Pardoned Financier Pledged Money to Clinton Library
Bush in First Step to Shrink Arsenal of U.S. Warheads
One Hurt as Car Bomb Goes Off in Orthodox District of Jerusalem

Current Events

Name _____   Date _____

Watch the news or read the newspaper with your family. Write
and draw about something that is important for us to know.

This is what the story I heard about looks like:

Who was involved in this story? _____

_____

What happened? _____

_____

_____

Is this good news or bad news? _____

Where did you hear about this?   Radio   TV   Newspaper

FIGURE 4.1

China Papers Say CNN Knew of Immolation
China Said to Punish Unionist
Russia Vows to Start Destroying Chemical Arms
Church's Window on the Past, and the Future
Congress Plans Study of Voting Processes and TV Coverage
Happily in the Middle
Washington Opera Gets Gift for Training Program
South Carolina Governor Honors 3 killed in 1968
A Telescopic Lens on a Baseball Legend
Columbia Takes Wraps off Seminar with Gore
The Pardons Look More Sordid (editorial)
Bipartisanship on Patients' Rights (editorial)
Cracking Down in Zimbabwe (editorial)
Poor and Homeless: Seeking a Way Out (letter to the editor)
The Battle Over a Tax Cut is Joined (letters to the editor)
Fix Up School Buildings (letter to the editor)
Hearing the Voices of Hip-Hop (op-ed article)

Section B (The Living Arts)

Trolling and Scavenging to Fill Empty Bellies
The Story of the Interned Jewish Refugees

Section C (Business & Sports)

Kevin Garnett of the Minnesota Timberwolves is the Focus of a Campaign for *And 1* Sneakers (Business)
Stern Concerned by Problems On and Off the Court (Sports)
It's More Program Than Pro (Sports)
Glickman Demanded Quality (Sports)

Let's briefly look at three articles. I've chosen "Cosmetic Saves a Cure for Sleeping Sickness" (McNeil, 2001), "China Said to Punish Unionist" (Eckholm, 2001), and "Hearing the Voices of Hip-Hop" (Sanneh, 2001). These articles can be the subject of a class discussion or debate, used with journal writing, shaped into research projects, or be a part of a larger unit or topic a class is already studying. They could also be used for two activities that I describe later, "Take a Stand" and "Four Corners." I primarily look at them here in the context of writing and discussion, suggesting some of the questions these articles can help students and teachers explore.

"Cosmetic Saves a Cure for Sleeping Sickness"

Sleeping sickness is one of the most devastating diseases in Africa. The disease is caused by the bites of tsetse flies and "drives victims mad before killing them." About 300,000 Africans get sleeping sickness every year. For ten years the drug eflornithine has been a "miracle cure" for the disease. Large drug companies have been making the drug in the hope that it could be used to fight cancer—and make them a lot of profit. However, they finally decided it had no future with cancer, so they stopped making the drug, even though it could save tens of thousands of Africans every year. Since most African nations are poor, they couldn't pay for the drug. But then the drug company was surprised. They discovered that the drug prevents facial hair growth in women, so they started making it again as a face cream for women.

By exploring the actions of businesses and corporations children can ask powerful questions to consider the behavior of companies—which can then be connected to their own behavior. In this situation the drug company is willing to make the drug for affluent women to buy as a cosmetic, but they were going to stop making a "miracle drug" that could save thousands of poor Africans who can't pay for it, or pay enough for it. Students could explore questions such as: Should drug companies be strictly for profit? Is there such a thing as too much profit? What if the CEO of the drug company is being paid millions of dollars a year? Do the United States and the rest of affluent world have any responsibilities to the poor and sick of the world? Do we, as individuals, have any responsibilities toward the poor and sick? How many billions of dollars do Americans spend on cosmetics each year? How about video games? Pet supplies? Fast food? What are our priorities as individuals, societies, and nations? What can we do? What should we do?

"China Said to Punish Unionist"

This is a short article about Cao Maobing, a factory worker at the Funing County Silk Mill in Jiangsu Province, China. Cao tried to form an independent labor union at his factory (as opposed to the typical government-controlled union). One day after he spoke with reporters from the *New York Times* and *The Washington Post*, he was taken to a psychiatric hospital by the police, and later forcibly drugged and given electroshock. The hospital director told the *New York Times*, "Mr. Cao suffers paranoid psychosis." The New York organization, Human Rights in China, protested, saying that Cao is not mentally ill. To protest his arrest, Cao started a hunger strike.

By exploring the behaviors of governments children can question issues of goodness, decide on what they believe is the appropriate behavior, roles, and standards for government, and connect those same standards to themselves. Some of the questions that can be written about, discussed, and researched with this article are: Why would the government of China put an apparently healthy man in a psychiatric hospital? What are your opinions of labor unions? What is the history of unions and resistance to unionizing in our own country? What are the moral and political connections between what China did to Cao Maobing and what the affluent factory owners (such as Andrew Carnegie and Henry Ford) did to their workers in the early twentieth century? Where else is this happening in the world? Is it happening in our country now? What about the fact that Americans buy many of the products made in Chinese factories (and factories in other "third world" countries), with conditions and pay far below the United States' standards and laws? Is it okay for American companies to use labor and environmental practices in other (typically poor) countries that are not allowed in the United States, such as denying workers the right to unionize? Would you be willing to pay twenty dollars more for gym shoes if it meant the factory workers earned a livable wage? Is it okay for corporate executives to make millions of dollars, sometimes hundreds of millions of dollars, each year? Should we care about factory workers in China? Migrant farm workers in California? Minimum wage workers at McDonalds? What should we do to promote freedom and economic justice in other countries?

Being good is helping children to see that we have connections to all people. Simply being human and living on the same planet and breathing the same air connect us. And we are connected morally—that is, we should all promote the common good. As Nel Noddings (1992) advocates, we need to help children to *care*, and that includes caring about strangers, even if they live five thousand miles away. But we are also connected more directly because we buy things that are manufactured by workers all around the world, fruits and vegetables that are picked by migrant farm workers in our own country, and hamburgers that are flipped by minimum wage workers at fast food restaurants. Being critical of how we spend, invest, and make our money is being good.

"Hearing the Voices of Hip-Hop"

This is an op-ed article from the *New York Times* about the popular rap singer Eminem, who had been criticized for the content of his songs on his "Marshall Mathers LP" CD. The author, Kelefa Sanneh, calls his lyrics "repugnant," saying, "His lyrics are a barrage of invective: he refers to women and gay people with the crudest of slurs, and he seems to view murder and rape as recreational activities." However, she also calls him a "genius," adding, that his songs have "good" lyrics that purposely contrast with the "bad" lyrics. She writes, "The album doesn't sound like a diatribe; it sounds more like a ferocious argument among a motley cast of characters. The result is a masterpiece of wit and paranoia, where no provocation goes unanswered and none of the characters come out clean." To make the controversy more complex (and more interesting) Eminem's CD was nominated for Album of the Year by the Grammy Awards. Sanneh writes, "This year's controversy is a credit to the [Grammy] academy: they have acknowledged that sometimes great pop music is greatly offensive."

This is a perfect article to have kids think about their own opinions of what is morally good and bad. Popular music is situated in many of their lives. What are their thoughts about Eminem's CD? (I might play certain parts or songs of the CD and/or read some of the lyrics for middle school kids. This can be explored with intermediate-aged kids without listening to the CD or reading the lyrics. A teacher can also choose to just talk about the issues.) Should people be allowed to write and perform any song they want? Should we have freedom of speech even if a song is offensive, even racist and sexist and violent? Should Eminem perform the song on the Grammy Awards with kids watching? Should he win a Grammy? Do we agree with Sanneh's point, that music (or any kind of visual art or drama or writing) can be offensive but can still be great art? Do we know of any other examples? Should there be age limits on buying explicit CDs, like there are age limits for buying alcohol and cigarettes?

Magazines

Stop at any newsstand or magazine rack and you are standing before a wealth of content and issues for children to explore. Mainstream news magazines such as *Time* and *Newsweek* can be good sources; however, I strongly recommend going beyond mainstream magazines, which are limited in their scope and perspective and coverage of social justice and moral issues. Here are fifteen good magazines, each with their own political ideology:

The New York Times Magazine	*Harper's*
The New Yorker	*Mother Jones*
The Nation	*The Weekly Standard*
The Atlantic Monthly	*The Progressive*
The Utne Reader	*The National Review*
Ms.	*The New Republic*
In These Times	*Adbusters*
National Geographic	

Some people would say that these magazines are too political and literary to use with children. First, it's good that they're political. Remember, how we behave and how we see our roles in society and the classroom are political and social issues. Second, these magazine articles are highly intellectual and sometimes controversial, and if we want to encourage our students to really think and care about important issues, then we need to allow them and challenge them and trust them to do exactly that. Third, many of these articles are difficult to read, but students don't have to read an article to benefit from it. When *The Atlantic Monthly* had an article on child labor in poor countries I brought it into my classroom and shared it with my elementary students. I showed them the pictures and read them some of text, and we had a good discussion. Finally, some articles are actually rather short and can be read by students starting in fourth or fifth grade. Teachers can also read short articles aloud to their class. Here are two examples of magazine articles that could help children think about behavior and character and how we treat others.

"The Singer Solution to World Poverty"

Peter Singer (1999) is a controversial philosopher who suggests that the middle class (and wealthy) in affluent countries are living a life of luxury when they could be giving much of their money to save the lives of deeply impoverished children around the world. Singer writes that most Americans could live on $30,000 a year and perhaps should give the rest of their money to organizations such as Oxfam, which works to help the poorest people in the world. Singer challenges readers by asking if the next time they go out to dinner they should, instead, eat dinner at home and give the dinner money to save these children. I would easily share this article with students in fourth or fifth grade and above. I'd be very interested in students' responses to Singer's arguments. I could ask, for example: What would you be willing to give up (a video game, eating out with your friends, your bike, clothes, etc.) to help poor people? Is it okay that we have very rich countries and very poor countries? What are wealthy countries doing to help poor countries? What should they be doing? What can we do? Do we have any obligations to help poor people? All of these questions can be used to help kids look inward and form their moral identity (Glover, 1999), which helps to shape their behavior.

"The Conscience of Place: Sand Creek"

This is a short article by Verlyn Klinkenborg (2000) on the Sand Creek Massacre, one of the worst massacres of Native Americans in our country's history. The article could be read by middle school students (it may be a bit graphic for younger kids), such as a part of an American history or Native American unit in seventh or eighth grade. (It can still be shown or read aloud to younger students.) On November 29, 1864, Colonel John Chivington of the Colorado Cavalry led 725 men in a "slaughter" of between 125 and 160 Cheyennes and Arapahos. Most of those murdered were women, children, and the elderly. When the killing ended, the soldiers mutilated the bodies and burned their lodges. The year before the Sand Creek Massacre two of its Cheyenne victims, War Bonnet and Standing in the Water, had visited the White House. Abraham Lincoln addressed them: "It is the object of this government to be on terms of peace with you, and with all our red brethren. We make treaties with you, and will try to observe them; and if our children should sometimes behave badly, and violate these treaties, it is against our wish."

Some of Colonel Chivington's men objected to the massacre—calling it "murder"—and in an excellent example of being good, Captain Silas Soule refused to participate, and later testified against Chivington during an investigation. This article is a much more honest depiction of Native American history than in social studies textbooks (Loewen, 1994). It can be used to help children understand the immoral scope of their treatment, to debate within themselves and with others what this should mean for us today. I would ask students what responsibility Abraham Lincoln had for the massacre, and what they might do today in response. Students could work in groups to design a memorial for the Sand Creek Massacre.

There are also magazines written specifically for children, such as, *The Weekly Reader, Junior Scholastic,* and *Time for Kids.* These publications can cover excellent issues for children to read and talk about. For example, the April 9, 2001, issue of *Junior Scholastic* had a cover story on child labor. However, they can also be simplistic and not include multiple perspectives to their stories. That same article has nothing to say on child labor in the United States, or that U.S. consumers buy many products made by child labor in other countries. The article implies that child labor is strictly a "third world" problem. So while these magazines can be valuable to use, we need to be critical of them and seek out other sources. There are also many excellent independent magazines (known as "zines") available at some newsstands, as well as "e-zines" available on the Internet.

Special Projects

Once again I want to be up front regarding the large curriculum teachers are expected to teach within a limited period of time. The content—usually in the form of textbooks—can be overwhelming. Still, even given these expectations, I encourage teachers to try to make time for some "extra" projects, and these can include projects specifically created to help kids explore issues of goodness, character, and social justice. Later in this chapter I suggest ways teachers can integrate being good into typical school subjects, but here I want to advocate the idea of creating projects in addition to those from the "official curriculum" (although some of that content could also be integrated into these projects).

I've done some of these projects with my students. A class of fourth- and fifth-graders did a project on equality and prejudice that included researching an injustice and making a class presentation on it. (The kids chose to study class cliques, African Americans and whites, sexism, treatment of the elderly, and ant-Semitism.) We also discussed newspaper articles about equality (and inequality) and prejudice, which helped my students see how pervasive these injustices are in the world. Another class studied smoking, looking, for example, at how advertising tries to get people (and kids) to smoke. All of these topics have issues of morality, character, and goodness imbedded in them. At their best these projects are not just about the facts of sexism or smoking, but include what these issues and facts mean to each student and how they can help students shape the kind of people they want to be.

Most of these projects would be long-term, lasting from two to three weeks, all the way up to six or seven weeks. While it may seem difficult to find the time to do an extra project, I really believe most teachers could do it if they wanted to (especially if they're in a self-contained classroom and teach the same kids all day). They just need to find the time. I suggest three to five days a week for at least an hour a day. Here are five more project ideas:

1. Study the toy industry. How are toys created and marketed? How do parents decide to buy toys? What are the connections between toys, television shows, movies, and fast food? Why do kids want certain toys? Why do most boys and girls want toys intended for their gender? Are there connections between toys and violence? Should we make and buy "war toys"? What toys do we own?

2. Study the media. How are different cultural groups, genders, and economic classes portrayed on TV? What shows do the kids watch? What commercials are attached to specific shows? How much time do we spend with media? How do commercials and print advertising try to manipulate people into buying things? Is it okay to manipulate people? How do television news shows report (or make) the news? What stories do they include and not include?

3. Study money. How much money do different people (locally, nationally, and globally) have? What have been the patterns of income levels over time? Where did money come from? How do people make their money? How do kids get money? What do they spend their money on? How do American adults spend their money? How important is money to people? How do the lotteries work? How does (and should) the government spend tax money?

4. Study the environment. What is the relationship between consumerism, the environment, and natural resources? How much of different natural resources do we use (compared to other countries)? How is

the American lifestyle impacting the environment? How are we working to save the environment? Where are we hurting the environment?
What animals and plants are endangered and what can we do to save
them? In what ways can we live a more environment-friendly life?

5. Study goodness. What does it mean to be good? Who do we know
    that we consider to be good and bad? Who are our role models from
    past and present? What do people think about goodness? Are most
    people good? Are people born good or must we make them good?
    How do people become bad? What can we do to be good people?

Classroom Peer Mediation

I taught at a school that had a peer mediation program with many positive results. The idea of peer mediation is actually simple, but it requires
having trust in children. Kids are trained to help their peers solve conflicts. In my school when two students had an argument or a fight, either
a teacher or another student suggested peer mediation. If both students
agreed, a form was filled out and given to the teacher who ran the program. Later that day the students were pulled from class and went to a
room with another student (a trained mediator) to sit and talk through
the conflict. The teacher sat within earshot of the mediation but did not
get involved unless it was necessary (which was rare). If they agreed, the
resolution was put in writing and signed by everyone.

Teachers can implement peer mediation in their own classroom. If
students have a conflict, they can go to a designated corner of the room
with a trained peer as mediator. The bigger ideas here are about solving
conflict peacefully and talking through a problem and listening to what
others have to say, which is all being good. An equally important benefit
of peer mediation is that by giving kids the opportunity to be mediators,
we are helping them to not only be good, but also be their best by helping others to be good. To start a classroom peer mediation program requires a serious commitment from a teacher, because being a good
mediator needs to be taught. But if a teacher makes the qualities of peer
mediation an important part of their classroom, then everyone is actually
benefiting from thinking about those qualities. And this can give a
teacher the opportunity to challenge a student who has had some behavior problems to become a peer mediator. Sometimes what these kids need
most is someone who trusts them to be good.

Good Angel, Bad Angel

I learned this idea from middle-school teacher Dan August. He uses it with children's literature, but it can easily be used with other scenarios. I'll use the children's novel, *Homeless Bird* (Whelan, 2000), to explain how it works. The book is about 13-year-old Koly, who lives in India and whose parents have arranged for her to be married. Koly struggles between expectations of her culture and family and her dislike for an arranged marriage. I don't want to give too much of the wonderful story away, but Koly does marry her arranged spouse, moves in with her in-laws, and goes on to have much conflict with her mother-in-law (her *sass*). To do Good Angel, Bad Angel a teacher chooses two students to role-play characters from the book, such as Koly and her sass. Four more students are chosen to role-play the "Angels." Each book character (Koly and her sass) has a good angel and a bad angel standing next to her. The rest of the class sits in front of or around them, observing and participating at some point. They discuss the book and a particular scene or moral descision the characters have or could make. As the facilitator the teacher poses questions, such as, "Koly, what are you thinking about this issue right now?" After Koly speaks the teacher then gets the opinions of Koly's Good and Bad Angels—which are really portraying Koly's conscience. Quite literally right before them the students are weighing moral decisions and considering different options. Interesting and provocative debates can happen: between the characters, between the angels, between characters and angels, as well as the give-and-take possibilities between the characters, the angels, and the rest of the student audience (as well as the teacher).

Good Angel, Bad Angel is a thoughtful—perhaps even fun way—for students to think through moral decision making. Beyond its use with children's literature, student's can portray "angels" for historical figures (and their decisions), current events, government policies, local issues (such as a law a city council is debating), and problems and moral dilemmas students themselves face in their lives (taking drugs, drinking alcohol, being in a clique, excluding kids on the playground, joining gangs, disrupting the classroom, etc.).

Movies, Music, Television, Video Games, and the Internet

Imagine some of the questions from the media that can be explored with children: Is violence okay in movies, television, music, and video games?

How much violence is too much violence? How about sex? How about drug use? Do violence and sex in the media influence violence and sex in society? Do the creators and artists of media have any responsibility to society? What role does money play in media? Should ethics and goodness take priority over profits? How are people—especially women, ethnic minorities, and the poor—portrayed in the media? In what ways might the media perpetuate social, cultural, and economic stereotypes? What are the roles of the media in a democracy? These questions can be discussed, written about, role-played, researched, and debated. I've had excellent discussions with my students on the ethics of manufacturing, marketing, and playing violent video games. I did not use this time to lecture about the evils of these games, but rather to facilitate a discussion to encourage my students to listen to what others had to say and to help them to question their own assumptions.

Movies are equally ripe for exploration. I had a class meeting with my fourth and fifth graders about movie advertisements. First, I wanted to help them understand how manipulative they can be. How the movie studios take reviewers' comments out of context, how they add exclamation points to their quoted blurbs, how they hype a movie before it opens, how they sometimes don't allow reviewers to pre-screen certain movies because they anticipate bad reviews, and how they have little-known movie reviewer "ringers" who will always give them a good line to quote in a movie ad. (Columbia Studios went even further, inventing their own fictitious movie reviewer to "quote" in their advertisements.) Second, I wanted my students to consider all of these issues from ethical and moral perspectives, asking themselves and debating if these are good and proper business practices. This discussion (which was framed around the opening—and the tremendous hype—of the movie "Godzilla") was a success, largely because movies are such a big part of children's lives, making our talk meaningful and relevant. We can also watch movies (and television shows) with our students and use them as springboards for exploring goodness.

Needless to say television is powerful. By the time typical children are five years old, they will have spent more time in front of a TV than they will spend in all of their years in a college classroom. By high school graduation they will have spent 22,000 hours of TV time, more than twice the time spent in school. An average American seventeen-year-old has seen more than 350,000 television commercials. Not only is the content of television loaded with issues and questions of goodness, the role of TV in our society—as well as how it portrays our society—is ripe for exploration. It can be especially thoughtful and critical to have kids look at how television shows (including the news) portray issues involving race, culture, class, gender, and the environment. Are they realistic? Are they honest? What is not on TV, and what stories and perspectives are not covered by the news? Having kids keep a TV journal for a week or two, recording everything they watch (including commercials and sports), can help students analyze and compare their viewing habits, the content of TV, and marketing practices. These journals can be compiled for the entire class and turned into graphs comparing, for example, what shows girls watch and what shows boys watch, or what commercials appear on what shows and why (helping students to understand the concept of being a target market). Students can survey other students and adults about their viewing habits. Discussions can be had not only about TV, but also on how we spend our time. If most of us weren't spending all that time in front of the television, what else could we be doing? What is a good use of our time?

The Internet, music, and video games offer further opportunities to have students think about being good. I had a class meeting with fourth and fifth graders about violence in video games (Wolk, 1998). Chris, a fifth grader, brought a copy of the video game magazine *Ultra Gameplayers* to school. Chris told me about a new video game called "Grand Theft Auto," where the player hijacks a car and goes on a violent crime spree. I used the review of the game in his magazine as the topic for discussion in our class meeting the next day. I read the review to the class and facilitated a heated discussion on the morality of the game as well as the people who make and market it. Interestingly the class was divided by gender, with the boys loving the game and the girls hating it. This shows how exploring one topic (violence in video games) can lead to exploring other topics (gender in society), and all done under the larger purpose of being good.

Teaching with Poetry

In Chapter 5 I write about using children's literature to teach for being good, but here I would like to write specifically about using poetry with children. I loved teaching with poetry. I did not emphasize my students learning the one "correct" interpretation of a poem, but rather the much more constructivist philosophy of what the poem means to them and how it may connect to their unique lives and experiences. In addition to writing poetry, I had my students (including my younger elementary-grade students) read great poets such as Gwendolyn Brooks, William Carlos Williams, Walt Whitman, Langston Hughes, e. e. cummings, Robert Frost, and Emily Dickinson. Kids can also read poetry connected to periods in history and cultures, such as poems by (and about) Native Americans, the Vietnam War, the Holocaust, and Civil Rights Movement, as well as poetry about nature and the environment. Linda Christensen (2000) writes:

> Poetry is held too sacred, revered a bit too much to be useful. Someone lied to us a long time ago when they whispered, "Kids hate poetry." Kids might hate the poetry that rustles in old pages and asks them to bow and be quiet when they come into a room. They might hate reading poetry unlocked only by the teacher's key and writing poetry that's delivered up like the *New York Times* crossword puzzle, but give them poetry that presses its ear against the heartbeat of humanity and they're in love. (p. 126)

Linda Christensen (2000) has written extensively on how she uses poetry in her classroom to teach for social justice. She has her students write poems about where they are from (with most stanzas beginning with "I am from . . ."); they write poetry from the perspective of oppressed people throughout history, giving them voice; they write poetry from the perspective of characters in novels; they read the poetry of activists and of poets from a wide variety of cultures. And at the end of each school year they write "Remember Me" poems about another student in the class. In explaining her use of the activist poetry of Martin Espada—and echoing the use of poetry for teaching goodness—Christensen writes:

> I use Espada's poetry, in English and in Spanish, to teach students how to use metaphors and how to write a "persona poem," but I also use Espada's poetry because he shows how to make visible the work of those who toil in physical labor. . . . Teaching students to respect the custodian who mops their halls, the short order cook who makes their tacos, or the field worker who picks their strawberries should be part of our critical classrooms. (pp. 139–140)

Nancy Gorrell (2000) writes about how she uses photography and art to inspire her students to write poetry. Her larger purposes, however, are to teach her students *empathy* and create a "curriculum of peace." For example, after showing her students a photograph from the Holocaust of a young Polish boy with his hands raised under the watchful eye of a Nazi soldier, she had her students write a poem to anyone in the picture. Some students wrote to the boy, others wrote to the German soldier, and others wrote to a woman standing next to the boy, also with her arms raised. After they shared and discussed their poems, Gorrell had her students write poems about an image (photograph, sculpture, a monument, another form of art) that they found and that "affects [them] profoundly." She gave her students the freedom to find images that were relevant and meaningful, and then used those connections to have the students write poetry in response.

Group Games and Play

Kids can learn a lot about being good from games and simply "playing." This can be done as class "free time," during recess, or as collaborative games with the entire class participating. First, games have rules; if you don't follow the rules, then you can't play the game (or at least it won't be very much fun or it won't "work"). Following the rules of a game is being good. Having kids talk about why it's important to follow the rules of games—and that this can be difficult at times—is also being good. Second, people need to get along to play a game (and enjoy it). Obviously "getting along" is being good. And finally, playing games is fun and can help nurture community, both of which are being good.

When students are playing kickball during recess or checkers during class free time, it is a great opportunity to teach kids about goodness. The old adage, "It's not whether you win or lose, but how you play the game," is part of the focus. Obviously we don't want to lambaste kids with the message, which would ruin the fun of the game. But a lot can be learned when kids are playing a game and being both bad and good. If students play "tag" at recess and there are no problems and everyone gets along, we can simply compliment them on how well they played. If there is a problem, perhaps three kids getting into an argument, it might be better to use that time to help the students think about their arguing rather than just to control the situation and "force" them to be good.

In her book, *You Can't Say You Can't Play*, kindergarten teacher Vivian Gussin Paley (1992) writes of her students repeatedly excluding other children in their play:

By kindergarten . . . a structure begins to be revealed and will soon be carved in stone. Certain children will have the right to limit the social experiences of their classmates. Henceforth a ruling class will notify others of their acceptability, and the outsiders learn to anticipate the sting of rejection. Long after the hitting and name-calling have been outlawed by the teachers, a more damaging phenomenon is allowed to take root, spreading from grade to grade. (p. 3)

So Paley initiated a new rule in her classroom, and hung a sign on the wall: "You can't say you can't play." Students were no longer allowed to exclude other students. Of course, as Paley noted, the rejection continued in their play, but this rule and their discussions about it would give her students an ideal to work toward, a way of thinking about what they *should do*. When a fifth-grade student in her school told Paley that her plan wasn't a good idea because children need to learn that exclusion is a part of life, she responded: "Maybe our classrooms can be nicer than the outside world" (p. 100). Paley was helping her students—teaching her students—to question what they assume to be true, that exclusion and rejection are "natural" and an acceptable fact of life. She wanted to challenge these students to rethink what it means to be good.

Class Rules

Once again I want to comment on class rules, suggesting a specific activity. At their best, class rules (or as I suggested previously, class values) will not only be a list of rules on a classroom wall, but also be an ongoing opportunity to learn about being good. As I suggested earlier, teachers can involve their students in writing class rules or values. This does not eliminate the need for clear expectations. Children do need to know what is and what is not allowable behavior in their classroom. Here's one way to do this: Within the first few days of school the students can be divided into small groups and each group can brainstorm a list of class rules and/or values. Each group is given a large sheet of butcher paper for writing their list of rules and values. Once finished the groups can hang up all the sheets together and compare them. They can look for common themes and ideas, and with the teacher's help, can merge the lists into one list. Teachers have a crucial role here. Not only are they the facilitators, but also they also need to make suggestions the kids don't make. If none of the groups included the rule, "be polite" or the value "promote the common good of our classroom," and teachers feel that is important, they should add it. And a value here is not just the end product of the list of rules. It is equally the *process* the class goes through to create the list. It is an open discussion where ideas and perspectives are shared, creating the perfect opportunity, for example, to talk about what the "common good" means.

This process requires time. As teachers we can't expect a class to seriously consider and debate possible class rules in fifteen minutes or half an hour. (For younger kids, perhaps below third grade, a half hour might work.) If we want quality thinking and quality work, teachers need to give their students quality time. For this entire process, I would allow a few hours (with some breaks). It could also be done over several days. By spending time doing this you're teaching kids that these ideas are important enough to spend the time, and that too is goodness.

Here is another idea for class rules. This one was done by my old junior high school (and is available at their website: www.sd68.k12.il.us/handbook/rights.html). They made a list called "A Student's Rights and Responsibilities," written side by side to connect the idea that with rights come responsibilities. Here are two:

RIGHTS	RESPONSIBILITIES
I have the right to be happy and to be treated with kindness in my school; this means that no one should laugh at me or hurt my feelings.	I have the responsibility to treat others with kindness; this means that I will not laugh at or tease others, or try to hurt the feelings of others.
I have the right to learn about myself and others at my school; this means that my opinions and feelings will be treated with respect and consideration.	I have the responsibility to learn about myself and others in this school; this means that I will listen to and respect the opinions and feelings of others.

The school (or actually the entire district) has two additional lists: one with the rights and responsibilities of teachers and another for the parents.

Take a Stand and Four Corners

A classroom activity that can structure good discussion and debate is "Take a Stand" (Schrank, 1972). Five signs are put on the floor in a horizontal line across the room: Strongly Agree, Agree, Neutral, Disagree, and Strongly Disagree. The teacher sets up a scenario, such as, "Carlos knows that his friend Eric is using drugs so he tells Eric's parents." The students then walk over to the sign they agree with and "take a stand." The students take turns debating the positions they have taken, and, most importantly, they are allowed to move to another "stand" at any time if they change their minds. The teacher can add information as the debate progresses. The teacher might add, "The drug Eric is using is marijuana." This might influence the students' opinions. Some students might at first agree that Carlos did the right thing telling Eric's parents, but then they could change their mind, saying that marijuana isn't serious enough to warrant that.

John Gaughan (1999) writes of using the activity "Four Corners" when his students were studying immigration and intolerance. After watching the movie, "El Norte," which is about two Guatemalan peasants seeking refuge through Mexico and the United States, his students took one of four positions on immigration policy and went to one of the classroom corners for discussion and debate. The positions were:

1. Illegal immigration should be stopped.
2. Illegal aliens with jobs should be permitted to stay.
3. Quotas should be raised so more people can immigrate legally.
4. Quotas should be lowered; the U.S. has too many new immigrants. (p. 317)

Four Corners can be used for everything from political policies to school and classroom rules, from problems (and possible solutions) in the local community to global injustices. All of these can be divided into different perspectives and opened up for serious discourse. Activities such as these can be expanded into research projects or activities such as having kids create symbolic murals explaining issues and stating their beliefs.

Debates

A debate can be done as part of a larger unit or it can be done to simply have a debate on topics in the news. Debates can be formal, which usually requires the students to do some research and planning, or they can be informal or spur of the moment. For example, my fourth and fifth graders were discussing the death penalty during a class meeting. The kids had passionate opinions about the topic so I split our rug in half and had the students choose a side, either for or against the death penalty. We spent the next half hour debating the topic, which obviously involves many issues of goodness, morality, justice, and economics. ("Take a Stand" and "Four Corners" are forms of informal debate.) The list of topics that a class could debate is limitless: gun control, the "War on Terrorism," searching kids' school lockers and book bags for drugs and weapons, specific laws, a ruling by the U.S. Supreme Court, the high pay of athletes, the meaning of "freedom of speech." By examining and questioning the goodness of others—their decisions and their actions—we are examining and questioning the goodness of ourselves.

During another class meeting the same fourth and fifth graders were discussing zoos. The discussion and the different perspectives brought up were so thoughtful that I decided on the spot to facilitate the making of a class list on the pros and cons of zoos:

ZOOS

Pro

- People can learn about animals, their habitats, nature, and the earth.

- We can actually see animals we otherwise could not see.

- People can see and learn about endangered animals and the political, economic, and moral issues about them; zoos can aid in their survival.

- Animals are now given more room to live and more "real" habitats.

- Zoos can research animals, increasing our knowledge of them.

- People can get exercise walking around a zoo.

- It's fun to go to the zoo.

- Zoos can increase our respect and appreciation for animals, nature, biology, and the earth (which can influence government policy decisions, as well as how we all choose to live and vote).

Con

- Even with "real" habitats animals still don't have enough room to live.

- Some zoos abuse animals.

- The animals' diets are not really natural.

- Zoos can smell bad.

- The animals are locked up, so they don't have freedom.

- The animals' environments and cages can be dirty.

- The animals' environments and cages are not natural.

- Some animals die in zoos.

- Zoos might teach people that humans should be in control of animals.

- Some zoos have animals do tricks, and maybe animals shouldn't be for human entertainment.

In the process of making this "debate list" my students were introduced to a variety of perspectives and opinions on zoos, including looking at zoos through a moral lens. As the kids sat on the floor in front of me, speaking about their ideas, I listed them on a large sheet of butcher paper taped to the chalkboard. A few of the points were mine; once again I did not shy away from offering my own thoughts, especially perspectives that my students did not think of, such as questioning the ethics of having animals, such as dolphins and birds, doing tricks for entertainment. Many of these ideas went against our own views about zoos, which hopefully encouraged all of us to make sense of new perspectives and shape an informed opinion. And maybe the next time some of us went to the zoo we saw it in an entirely new way.

Field Trips

Here are twenty field trips kids could go on to learn about being good: zoos, fire stations, police stations, courts, city hall and city council meetings, museums (science, natural history, art, and specialized museums such as the Peace Museum or the Holocaust Museum), plays, newspaper offices and printing plants, different ethnic neighborhoods, movies, exhibitions, restaurants, social service agencies, libraries, businesses, volunteer organizations and community centers, universities, historic sites, nature walks, and my all-time favorite, the sunrise. There is beauty and peace in watching the sun rise, and that is being extremely good.

Graphing Behavior

When I was teaching in a Chicago public school I had two classes. My morning class was a mixed fourth and fifth grade, and my afternoon class was a mixed third and fourth grade. (I taught language arts and social studies, and the students switched rooms after lunch with the teacher who taught math and science next door.) Both of these classes were the most challenging students I ever had concerning behavior. Some days were terrible, with students having screaming arguments; other kids had emotional difficulties with (thankfully, rarely) violent outbursts; many of the students turned in little homework (so I stopped giving it and had them do all of their work in class); and some of the students were just downright rude. The most frustrating behavior issue for me was the kids' constant interruptions of the classroom, from endless chitchat, to arguing, to yelling out a name at another kid or blurting out a joke. More than the "big" behavior problems, I struggled with the chronic "little stuff." Of course, this wasn't a problem with all of my students. Even given the classroom chaos at times, most of the kids had great behavior and were angry with the students who constantly disrupted our classroom.

I tried different ideas to solve these problems and had some success, but most of the interruptions continued. Every day I analyzed the situation, trying to figure out why this was happening. I wanted to understand the roots of the problem. I came to understand that some of the kids were so self-centered (or egocentric) and consumed by individualism that they had no idea how their behaviors were affecting the world beyond their bodies and their realities. I needed to show them what all of their little interruptions added up to. I needed to do something to help them see themselves. I decided to graph their interruptions.

I cut a four-foot by five-foot sheet of butcher graph paper and hung it on the wall. I wanted our graph to be very big. I drew two axes; the horizontal axis was the date and the vertical axis was the number of interruptions. It was a double line graph, with each of the two classes having a different color line. I purposely wanted each class to see how the other class was doing, hoping this would have a positive affect. Every day I kept count of the interruptions, no matter how small they were, with tally marks on the board. If a student yelled for another student to let him use his pencil, a mark went up; if a student whispered something to another student as I read a novel aloud to the class, a mark went up; if kids got into a shouting match, a mark went up. I wanted to help my students see several things:

- A lot of small interruptions add up to an endless large interruption.

- Some interruptions are worse then others, but an interruption is still an interruption and that means it's wrong.

- All of their interruptions negatively affect the learning of everyone in our classroom, and that hurts the common good of our classroom community.

- We all have the responsibility of thinking about the common good of our classroom. That means deciding to not blurt out a joke, even though we want to.

- I wanted to help my kids to see and *learn* that they were able to control their actions; they can have self-control if they choose.

- I wanted the graph to show the kids just how many interruptions we had every day. I wanted them to be *shocked*.

There is no question this was labor intensive. I accepted that going in. I knew that I'd be putting tally marks on the board all day, and that's exactly what I did. But I accepted the short-term disruptions of my teaching and their learning in exchange for what I hoped would be our long-term gains in behavior, thoughtfulness, and learning. Besides, with so many disruptions, what's the point of continuing with business as usual? Something had to change.

I tallied interruptions daily for about three weeks. At the end of each class (before lunch and at the end of the day) I totaled the marks and completed the graph, with the kids sitting before me. Here are the numbers of interruptions for both classes (read across), and remember that this is for only a half day of school, less than three hours:

| Morning Class: | 109 | 54 | 70 | 70 | 57 | 65 | 23 | 45 | 98 | 40 |
| | 45 | 60 | 70 | 53 | 39 | | | | | |

| Afternoon Class: | 87 | 42 | 30 | 30 | 37 | 80 | 84 | 21 | 45 | 68 |
| | 48 | 13 | | | | | | | | |

While I did not have any revolutionary success the numbers do show a downward trend. Both classes were shocked after the first day. None of the kids ever imagined that we had forty-two, much less 109 interruptions. We talked about this in our class meetings; some students spoke about being angry and how it was interfering with their learning. Most importantly the numbers showed the kids that they could—*if they wanted to*—have a day with much fewer interruptions. If they thought about self-control, cared about self-control, wanted self-control, then they could have self-control. School (and our classroom) didn't have to have lots of interruptions, which is what these kids were used to throughout much of their schooling. We were having them because certain kids were making certain bad decisions. We all needed to make good decisions, and decision making is one of the foundations of a democratic society (Engle & Ochoa, 1988).

Over the three-week period that I graphed the interruptions, I started having the class pick a goal for the number of interruptions for the day during each morning meeting. Three kids would suggest a number and I would pick a reasonable compromise. I did not hesitate to pick thirty or forty-five interruptions; I had to begin where the kids were and I was looking for improvement, not perfection, which I knew was unrealistic. As Martin Haberman (1995) writes, I understood that these kinds of problems were part of my job and I accepted that and worked with them. Having the goals helped the class to keep their interruptions down and to be good. It focused them and helped them to see that they did have control over their actions.

Mock Trials

I've done a few mock trials with my students. We put King George III on trial as part of a unit on the American Revolution. The students chose and researched roles, with two pairs of students as the prosecution and the defense teams. Mock trials can be highly thoughtful, extremely enjoyable, and a terrific opportunity to look at being good. They also require a lot of work for the teacher. Here are five mock trials that teachers can use to explore being good:

1. The United States' role in the Vietnam War
2. Fairy tales (for example, the wolf in the Three Little Pigs)
3. A company on trial for their products, such as violent or sexist video games or cigarettes.
4. Historical figures such as Andrew Jackson and his role in the conquest of Native Americans; Andrew Carnegie and the treatment of his workers in his steel mills; or Thomas Jefferson, who wrote that "all men are created equal," but who also owned nearly 200 slaves.
5. The United States government putting Japanese Americans into internment camps during World War II.

Mock trials can help children look at life from multiple perspectives, be critical, and to ask themselves what they believe is right and good. Here are a few suggestions for putting on a mock trial:

- For most kids in fourth grade and up, block out at least five weeks. This is assuming you work on the trial for at least one hour a day. This is also assuming the students already have some knowledge of the trial issue and context (for example, for a trial on the Trail of Tears the students will have to have general knowledge on the event as well as on life in the United States in 1838).

- For students in first to third grade, a trial can be simplified, taking anywhere from one to four weeks.

- Start with some mini-lessons and demonstrations on how a trial works. If need be, simplify it. Try and connect this to your students' existing knowledge of crime, the court system, lawyers, judges, and so on. Remember, some of what your kids know on these topics is wrong, especially since much of that knowledge comes from television and movies, but you can use that existing knowledge to help them learn.

- Assign (or have kids choose) roles. I'd suggest having two students each for the defense team and the prosecuting team. Assign a judge (or you be the judge). These kids need to do a lot of research on the overall issue. Make a list with the entire class of possible witnesses. Assign students to be these witnesses. They need to research the issue and their specific role. Some kids can create fictional characters, such as a Nebraska homesteader during 1838. Remaining students are the jury, and they, too, can create fictional characters. They also need to do general research on the topic. I'd let kids spend at least three weeks doing research (during class time), while the teacher has conferences with kids to help. Have due dates for research notes, and structure different parts of the trial preparation.

- Teachers need to help both teams of lawyers shape their cases and encourage all kids to take their parts seriously.

- Encourage students to dress up for their parts.

- Maybe videotape the trial to look at later.

Drama and Role-Play

I love using drama in the classroom. Done well, plays, skits, role-plays, and monologues are intellectual, fun, and thoughtful. They are a great way to integrate writing into any subject and nurture classroom community, and are an excellent medium to explore goodness in our lives and in our world. They also give kids the opportunity to get up and *move*, and that's important, because their biology tells them to move. Drama puts children's endless energy to good use, and that helps them to be good.

Drama can be used to act out events in history, such as slavery and the Underground Railroad, the Civil Rights Movement, and labor uprisings. Bob Peterson (2001a) writes of having his fifth graders role-play the U.S. Constitutional Convention, but with one major twist: having students play people who were not allowed to take part in the actual convention, such as slaves, women, and Native Americans. Drama can be a particularly powerful way to explore issues of social justice, such as economic inequality, sexual discrimination, and prejudice, as well as environmental abuses. Students can also dramatize events, scenes, and ideas involving goodness and character from their own lives, their communities, and the school and playground. For example, younger students can use drama to examine a student being teased on the playground and what they could choose to do in response. Students can also research and then role-play or do monologues of their heroes or people they feel have helped to make the world a better place, bringing them to life in the classroom. Bill Bigelow (2001) writes of teaching his students about "unsung heroes." The staple of school and textbook heroes typically includes George Washington, Abraham Lincoln, Thomas Jefferson, and Betsy Ross. Culturally diverse heroes are often limited to Martin Luther King Jr. and Rosa Parks. In great contrast to this, Bigelow introduces his students to Elizabeth Cady Stanton, Marcus Garvey, Jackie Robinson, Cesar Chavez, Sarah and Angelina Grimke, Fannie Lou Hamer, and William Lloyd Garrison, among many others. One of the very best ways we can encourage kids to be good is to help them learn about people from all walks of life who have been good. And dramatizing their goodness is one way to bring them to life in the classroom.

A Thoughtful Life

I adapted the idea of "A Thoughtful Life" from two great teachers, Kim Day and Diana Shulla (Wolk, 1998). They call their idea, "A Disciplined Life." Both ideas work the same way. I made a list of characteristics or habits of mind that are "good." I wrote each one in large letters on a piece of 6" x 18" cardboard and put them on the wall around a large handwritten sign that read A THOUGHTFUL LIFE. I had twenty-five characteristics and put them on the wall, where they stayed all year:

Be Helpful	Be Responsible	Create Art
Seek Wisdom	Ask Questions	Have Dreams
Promote Peace	Be Critical	Think for Yourself
Make a New Friend	Improve Yourself	Thank Someone
Practice Empathy	Be Open-Minded	Engage in Dialogue
Love Yourself	Write Something	Be Kind
Celebrate Differences	Think Before You Act	Be a Giver
Take Time to Listen	Do the Right Thing	Appreciate Nature
Read a Book		

These qualities of living a thoughtful life (some of which came from Kim and Diana) became an important part of our classroom culture. I wanted them to be as much a part of our classroom curriculum as reading and math. Every day, in a variety of contexts, some of these habits of mind came up—usually because I brought them up. If three kids were having a good discussion about a book in reading workshop, I might have praised them for "engaging in dialogue"; if a student was teasing another student, I might have used that to facilitate a discussion about "being kind" at our daily class meeting; if a student stopped two kids from fighting, I might have announced to the class how proud I was of that student for "promoting peace." All of these ideas are about goodness, and they can become a natural part of a classroom culture. These ideas can be used with journal writing, too. For example, you can have the class write about a characteristic or habit of mind that isn't on the wall and why they think it should be, or kids can write about a time they "thought before they acted," when they "appreciated nature," or about someone they know who reads books or is open-minded.

Integrating "Being Good" into School Subjects

Being good can be a part of every school subject. Teachers can integrate this content into topics that they are already teaching. Math and science, which are typically taught in a more rote and fact-based way than social studies and language arts, offer endless opportunities for teachers to use these disciplines to engage their students in conversations on morality, social justice, and the critical decision making necessary by an involved citizenship. Teachers can ask themselves why math textbooks have students graph pieces of candy—something that people never do in real life and is ultimately meaningless—rather than create graphs that have real meaning, such as what television shows students watch, how students spend an allowance they may get, or pollution levels around the country. The former is just an exercise while the latter ideas allow further explorations, such as talking about what patterns emerge (by age, gender, etc.) in TV watching, or how kids choose to spend their money, or how we're doing with taking care of our environment, three ideas that can be extended into being good.

Below I list each school subject with five ways to integrate goodness at various grade levels. (Language Arts is integrated throughout, and the following chapter is devoted entirely to reading.) At their best these would be taught as longer integrative projects.

Science

- My friend Chuck Cole taught middle school science for more than thirty years. He had his seventh graders read the book *Hiroshima* (Hersey, 1956) when they studied "atoms" and "atomic theory." Hersey's book is the famous account of dropping the atomic bomb on Hiroshima, told from the perspective of Japanese people. Chuck had his students read the book aloud in class for them to consider the typically "scientific" study of atoms from moral, cultural, and political perspectives. He had his students do a lot of writing in reaction to the book, emphasizing their personal meanings from the book. For example, two of the questions they responded to were: "In what way would you say you have changed as a result of reading this book?" and "How do you feel about the fact the U.S. dropped the bomb on Japan? Proud? Happy? Patriotic? Ashamed? Sorry? Glad? Etc. Describe your feelings and explain your point of view."

- In life science, students can explore different perspectives on genetic engineering. Should we, for example, alter the natural genetic structure of rice by adding vitamin A if it can prevent the death or blindness of hundreds of thousands of undernourished people around the world? Should we allow fish farmers to genetically alter salmon so they grow to market size sooner? Students can research and discuss how we (individually and collectively) treat living things, everything from flowers and trees to mammals and insects.

- Our society embraces technology and industry as progress, but what are the negative consequences of technology? Is there such a thing as too much technology or unethical technology? Is all technology progress? How might life be better without cars? Televisions? Microwave ovens? Cell phones?

- When studying electricity, even in the primary grades, ethical and social justice issues of energy use, conservation, and pollution can be discussed, debated, and researched. For example, should big cities keep so many lights on in their buildings at night when no one is inside them? Is our personal energy use in U.S. homes, which has increased 1,700 times since 1949, too much? What is good energy use? Is playing a video game a waste of energy if millions of people around the world don't have enough energy to fulfill their basic needs? What are the moral implications of the United States having only five percent of the world's population, yet using thirty percent of the world's resources?

- When exploring the human body, students can debate the "goodness" of marketing junk food to kids. Students can investigate being good and bad to our bodies. Older kids can discuss body image, and what our society (and the media) portray as a "good" body. Studying the human body can be connected to drug use and abuse, even extending into what are (or should be) good drug policies in the United States. Should drug abuse be considered a criminal problem or a medical and/or economic problem, which would require vastly different solutions?

Social Studies

- When studying slavery and the American Civil War, students can explore the goodness of abolitionists and the immorality of slave owners.

- When studying culture, kids can research, discuss, and write about racism, xenophobia, and prejudice, as well as the goodness of cultural diversity. Teaching for democracy, community, and social justice means creating an anti-racist and anti-oppression curriculum (Lee, 1995).

- When studying Native American history, students can consider what responsibilities the United States has to Native Americans today. Given the history of Native American genocide, and that today they have the highest rates of unemployment, alcoholism, and poverty in the country, does our nation have any obligations to them? For example, the Lakota Sioux have refused to collect an 800-million-dollar settlement for the Black Hills, instead waiting to get their land back (Frazier, 2000). Should we give the Black Hills back to them?

- Third and fourth graders typically study their city and state in social studies. This can include problems the city, state, and local community are having and need to be improved. By asking what is good and bad about our communities and states, we are making value judgments that reflect who we are. Students can research a problem (pollution, lack of local parks, gangs, unequal distribution of tax revenue, low voter turnout, the need to plant more trees, a better recycling program) and write an action plan for working to solve the problem. They can dramatize the problems with plays and skits.

- The U.S. Constitution opens up possibilities for issues of behavior, character, and social justice. For example, are the current amendments, such as the "right to bear arms," good? What exactly is "cruel and unusual punishment," and does the United States do a good job in interpreting (and acting on) that? What might be some new (and good) amendments? Is the structure of the government good, or might we make it better? How might we improve our system of voting? And how is our country doing constitutionally? Are we treating everyone equally? Does everyone have the same inalienable rights? What injustices is our country ailing from, and what can we do to heal them?

Math

- Design and create a blueprint of a new park for your neighborhood. What makes for a good park? Where should the park be located and why? What materials should we use? Should they be from recycled products?

- Survey people on social issues (poverty, gun control, tax cuts, health care, prejudice, etc.) and compute and graph the results (see Wolk, 1998).

- Compare present differences in salaries between men and women, as well as past salaries. Research and compute the percentages of representation in legislative bodies in the United States and around the world. How many women are in legislatures? How many African Americans, Latinos, Native Americans, and so on? Have students graph the gender and cultural makeup of the executives of the Fortune 500 corporations. (Peterson, 2001b).

- Survey and graph (and write about) the habits in life of the students in class, the kids in the school, or adults. How do kids spend their allowance? How do adults spend their money? How do we spend our time? What products and companies do we give our business to? How do we make these decisions? Even very young kids can do this using simple data collection and pictographs.

- Research and compare mathematical data from different cities, states, and countries: population, gross domestic product, poverty levels, education and literacy, levels of pollution, infant mortality, government spending, health care, prison population, labor practices, and specific data by income and ethnicity and gender. Much of this information is on the Web and available in inexpensive almanacs published annually. This can be especially powerful to do globally, comparing affluent countries with poor countries. (A great resource is the book *Material World* by Peter Menzel, 1999.)

The Fine Arts

- Create murals (especially symbolic murals) on various themes of goodness, behavior, and character. Create paintings and murals and other visual art in response to the ideas listed for science, social studies, and math.

- Have kids perform existing plays and plays they write themselves on topics of being good, especially from their own lives.

- Look at, discuss, and write about artwork that explores goodness, morality, and social justice, such as Picasso's "Guernica" on the Spanish Civil War, Lewis Hines' photographs of child labor, and Jacob Riis' photos and writings of "how the other half lives" in the turn-of-the-century slums. There is a lot of contemporary art that explores the morality of war, greed, prejudice, and so forth.

- Discuss and debate the value and role of art in society and a democracy. For example, should we use tax money to fund the arts? Why or why not? Debate former New York City Mayor Rudy Giuliani's controversial creation of a "decency panel" to create "decency" guidelines for art in publicly funded museums. Is this good or bad for democracy and freedom and art? Should art have limits?

- Have kids bring to class good music. Play diverse forms of music for students: classical, jazz, Native American, hip-hop, rap, swing, blues, rock, klezmer, and other lesser known music from a variety of local and global cultures.

Use Your Students' Lives

The more we can help our students make connections between the content of school and their lives, the more meaningful and relevant their learning will be. Just like adults, children experience issues, events, and decisions regarding goodness, behavior, character, social justice, and self-discipline every day. Take a moment and imagine all of the decisions you make in a typical day. Many of those decisions involve goodness: how we talk to people, how we spend our time, what we buy, how we drive, what we eat, how we raise our children, what we read, who our friends are, how we deal with anger and frustration, where we work and shop, and how we invest our money. We are constantly making decisions that are situated in values. How we live our lives, day to day, moment to moment, is a value and a moral statement. Perhaps the best way to teach being good is for us to see our students and their lives as curriculum. It is a way to show children that education is as much about knowing the facts about a war as it is about forming and defending an opinion on the morality of war, as much about learning about the world as it is about choosing how to live and act in the world, as much about learning about good people as it is about shaping our own goodness.

Here are five ways teachers can directly connect their students' lives to being good:

1. Have students interview a family member or friend who they think is a good person, perhaps even a role model. Have them write these as narratives and publish a class magazine.
2. Write autobiographies, including both good and bad decisions, actions, and experiences. Try to help kids write autobiographies that are more multidimensional and honest and that communicate the complexity and moral dimensions of life. (With help, younger kids could do this, too.)
3. Have students research their cultures and have a class "culture fair." Or have them write and illustrate picture books about their cultures and read them to younger kids. Learning about other cultures is being good.
4. For two weeks have students keep a log of how they spend their time (sleeping, watching TV, hanging out at the mall, talking on the phone, spending money, reading, etc.). Have them compute the percentages of how they spend their time (and perhaps money), create graphs, and write a reflective essay.
5. Have students make some form of "personal creation" (mural, multimedia presentation, painting, collage, sculpture, song, poetry, etc.) that communicates what they believe is most important in life.

Being Good Through Books

Reading is a basic tool in the living of a good life.
—Mortimer J. Adler

People read for many purposes. Our reading can give us pleasure, allow us to live vicariously, teach us about the world, answer our questions, give us insights into the wonders and complexities of life, enlighten us with knowledge in our interests from politics and baking to postmodern art and physics, and help us—hopefully—to become better people. My last point, reading to become better people, is usually lost when it comes to "school reading," which is, sadly, still dominated by textbooks and basals and worksheets. In school the purposes of reading are usually to have students improve their "comprehension skills" and "vocabulary" and to pass tests. This reduces reading to a mechanical and rote exercise, removes the pleasure and humanness from reading, and does little to help children learn how reading can shape who we are and make us better people. Books can help all of us to be good.

First is the question of why teachers should use real books, or what is commonly referred to as literature-based reading, rather than textbooks and basals. Here, in an oversimplified way, are some of the important reasons:

- They are real, just like the books we read in real life. Learning is best when it is authentic.

- Real books are whole and place skills and knowledge in authentic contexts. Fictional books, such as historical fiction, embed factual knowledge into their stories.

- Real books tell good, interesting, exciting, complex, and complete stories. We enjoy stories and make sense of life through stories.

- There is an enormous selection of real books from which to choose, which increases the chances of kids connecting with books that they like.

- Real books come in all different levels of difficulty so books can be better matched to each child's unique reading development.

- If students really connect with books, there is a much better chance of their learning to like (even love) reading, as well as the content that they're reading.

- If kids like reading, they'll read more books, and if they read more books, they'll improve at reading and its incidental knowledge (writing, comprehension, vocabulary, spelling, subject matter knowledge, etc.).

- Real books are more accurate, honest, and emotional than textbooks.

- Using real books allows teachers to model being real readers.

- Real books allow children to make connections to their real writing.

- It is easier to make our teaching culturally relevant with real books, which open up wider opportunities for teachers to choose books that connect to their students' cultures.

Granted, literature-based reading has less traditional structure than following a predetermined scope and sequence of a textbook series. But using real books can be just as structured and have just as high expectations (even higher) than using a textbook. (For more on literature-based reading, see Atwell, 1998; Calkins, 2000; Hynds, 1997.)

Good teaching with real books isn't as simple as having kids read the books. Having literature-based reading in a classroom is equally about what teachers choose to have their students do with those books, and how books and reading are presented to kids. Too often even real books are "basalized"; this just replaces a textbook or a basal with a novel, and turns a real book into a rote experience. The opposite of this—which is situated in a whole language, constructivist, and sociolinguistic belief system—is seeing that what matters most when reading a book isn't the text on the page, but the meaning that each reader constructs from his or her interaction with the text on the page. One hundred people reading *Charlotte's Web* will—and *should*—construct different meanings from the book. This is constructivism, the belief that people do not learn by placing neutral knowledge into empty heads, but rather by constructing our own sense of the world. Our unique self, including our existing knowledge, acts as a kind of "filter" to our consciousness. As we live (read a book, look at art, engage in conversation, watch a sunset) each of us constructs our own meaning. Classrooms that are more democratic are constructivist; they want to nurture these meanings, exploit them, share them, and use them to help children learn.

So, learning to be good from books isn't about kids "getting" the "correct" point or theme or facts of a book, but having them engage in their own transactions with books, make personal connections, and reflect on their own meaning making. Twenty-eight students reading the same novel or picture book should have many *different* reactions and connections to the book. This does not eliminate either the author's voice (or purposes) or the teacher's perspective. I used literature extensively in my classrooms, and I did not refrain from voicing my own ideas about a book to my students. When I read a book aloud to my class I always had specific ideas and content that I wanted my students to consider. I couldn't assume my students would "get" or even see a particular point (on being good or a point related to social justice, for example) from a book. A large part of my job as a teacher was to pull these ideas out of books for my students to think about, write about, talk about, and grapple with. What meanings these had for them was for each child to decide, but they could not even consider the ideas if they did not see them in the first place. So, while this is a constructivist philosophy, it wasn't only about having my students read books and tell me what they meant to them. I also wanted our reading to be an intellectual and communal experience, and that meant helping my students to think in new ways, and some of those ways had to do specifically with being good.

There are different ways to structure literature-based reading in a classroom. Here are six ideas:

1. independent reading with kids choosing their own books
2. literature circles or book groups with either all the students reading the same book, each group reading completely different books, or each group reading different books that are connected by a common theme
3. reading in pairs
4. whole class reading with everyone reading the same book
5. teacher reading a book (novel, nonfiction, picture books) aloud to the class
6. students reading picture books aloud to the class, in small groups, or to younger kids

For a literature-based classroom to be meaningful, students should spend at least thirty minutes a day in class reading, and a teacher should read aloud at least twenty minutes a day. To use books specifically to help kids to be good doesn't require any special reading time. Just as with the rest of the curriculum, it will be an everyday part of whatever books are being read in a classroom. I did, at times, select a book to read aloud specifically because it had potential for my students to explore issues of goodness, character, and social justice.

Of course, using books to be good doesn't stop once a book is completed. Teachers can have their students engage in a wide variety of activities and projects while they're reading their books and once they've finished them. Here are a dozen ideas on what teachers can have students do with books to explore being good:

• Have kids write letters in their journals about their books, and you (the teacher) can write back, and their classmates and parents can write back.

• Write and perform plays, skits, and role-plays, especially connecting ideas from books to the kids' lives. Have kids write or perform scenes that are *not* in a book they read so they'll consider how various characters would have acted.

- Have whole-class or small-group open discussions and debates.

- Write and illustrate picture books on how a book relates or connects to a student's life.

- Connect books (especially nonfiction and historical fiction) to studying historical and ethical events, actions, and decision making.

- Connect books to current events at the local, state, national, and global levels having to do with goodness and ethical behavior.

- Integrate the visual arts and have kids create murals, collages, photography, videos, and paintings from books. I especially like having kids create *symbolic* art in response to books.

- Have each student create a new book cover expressing his or her own meaning about an issue of goodness in a book. After reading poems by Langston Hughes, my students designed covers for a book of his poetry, expressing their outrage at racism.

- Write and give surveys on themes from books or interview people on those issues, and then graph and/or write up the results.

- Find connections between books and people (living or dead), research them, and then create something to show what they learned and what they think of the person.

- Have kids make an original "creation" to show what meaning a book had for them (poetry, visual art, computer multimedia, mixed media, etc.).

- Create presentations for younger students on ideas from books. For example, after reading Langston Hughes' poetry, my students could have written and performed puppet shows about racism for younger kids.

As teachers one of the most important things we can do is to help our students connect books to their lives. These connections do not have to be literal. If a teacher is reading *Freedom's Children* (Levine, 1993) (which is a collection of oral histories of children who were civil rights activists in the 1960s) to the class, the kids do not have to be civil rights activists (or activists at all) for them to connect to the book. We can help children make *conceptual* and *thematic* connections. For *Freedom's Children* we could have students do any of the following:

- Research a civic issue, problem, or controversy they're passionate about (and take a stand on the issue and come up with some ideas to improve them).

- Write/discuss if they have ever been an activist (or "active") for anything in any way.

- Discuss what cause or issue they might want to be an activist for now.

- Do an interview or survey on why people choose to be activists, or interview an activist.

- Research an activist from the past or present whom they respect.

- Write/discuss if they have ever been a victim of prejudice.

- Write/discuss what they think of our country's past and present racism and why racism still exists.

- Create a symbolic mural on racism and prejudice.

- Research current injustices in our country (or the world) that they feel strongly about.

- Have students write how the lives and stories of these children relate to their lives; have they had any similar experiences and feelings (Peterson, 1994)?

- Read, dramatize, and write about (and perhaps rewrite) fairytales to look at issues of goodness (even with older kids).

- Collect oral histories of people who lived through the Civil Rights Movement and write up their stories as a class magazine.

All of these ideas can do three things: They are situated in Levine's book; they relate that book conceptually to the kids' lives, experiences, opinions, and interests; and they raise issues of goodness, behavior, character, social justice, citizenship, and democracy. Put all of these together in a thoughtful and caring way and we can use *Freedom's Children* to encourage children to look inward, think about who they are and what they value, and become better people.

I am also a huge advocate of using picture books when teaching kids in *all* grade levels. I've taught every grade from third through eighth and used picture books in all of them (and in my college classes, as well).

Many picture books have deeply intellectual, emotional, and critical themes that can be a catalyst for serious discussion and exploration. I've used picture books with themes on racism, sexism, war, peace, the environment, economics and poverty, homelessness, cultural diversity, and so forth. The possibilities with picture books are endless! Kids can read picture books individually, in pairs, in book groups, and to younger students. Teachers can read them aloud, put them together as text sets by author or theme (as part of a unit or author study), or place them around the room in different centers. Teachers can integrate picture books across their curriculum and connect them to current issues in the news. A teacher can start using picture books simply by reading one book a week aloud to the class and the kids responding to them through journal writing and/or discussion. Here are five very thoughtful ways to use picture books:

1. Read a picture book and have the kids write just one word in response to it. Have them show their words and explain why they chose them.
2. Have kids create posters to "market" a solution to a social problems that's presented in a picture book. Hang the posters around the school or community.
3. Have kids write about how a book's characters, settings, issues, and plots connect to their lives, such as how a character is similar to someone they know.
4. Have kids create a new cover for the book, one that symbolizes an important theme in the book or a personal connection they made to the book.
5. Have kids act out scenes from a picture book. Or have them dramatize a theme of a book that has relevance to their own lives.

Following are five lists of books. The first three are lists of picture books, novels, and nonfiction books that can be used with students ranging from kindergarten to eighth grade (and beyond). The fourth list is of books written for adults that teachers can read to think about our own goodness, and the final list is of books on education that can help teachers think about being good, and what that might mean for our practice and the role of schooling in society. Maxine Greene (1988) wrote, "A teacher in search of his/her own freedom may be the only kind of teacher who can arouse young persons to go in search of their own" (p. 14). The same is true for being good. As educators and citizens, to arouse our students to goodness we must participate in our own ongoing journey of being good.

Fifty Picture Books

The Auction by Jan Andrews. An aging widower tells his grandson about his life on the family farm as he is preparing to sell it at auction.

When Sophie Gets Angry—Really, Really Angry by Molly Bang. Sophie gets very angry and decides to do what's best: remove herself from the situation, go for a walk in nature, and calm down.

Through My Eyes by Ruby Bridges. Ruby Bridges, the first African American girl to desegregate Alabama schools, tells her story of breaking the racist barrier.

Voices in the Park by Anthony Browne. The story of four people going to a park, with each person telling of the experience from their perspective. Browne gives each of the four people (actually, portrayed as gorillas)— a man and his daughter and a woman and her son—their own personality, while confronting issues of class. This may be the perfect book to help kids explore the idea of perspective.

Piggybook by Anthony Browne. A father and his two sons (gorillas again) do not appreciate the hard work of their mother. A great book to explore issues of gender (as well as appreciation and responsibility) with even the youngest students.

Between Earth & Sky by Joseph Bruchac. Little Bear, a Native American, learns about Native American sacred places from his uncle Old Bear. The book explains what Native Americans call the "seven directions." Bruchac is Native American and has written many books about his culture.

Going Home by Eve Bunting. A migrant farm family, living a difficult life on a strawberry farm, travels to their small home village, La Perla, Mexico, for Christmas.

Smokey Nights by Eve Bunting. A story during the Los Angeles riots after the Rodney King verdict. Daniel and his mother must escape the madness of the riots while unexpectedly making some new friends.

Someday a Tree by Eve Bunting. People join together to try and save an old oak tree that has been poisoned by chemicals.

Fly Away Home by Eve Bunting. A boy and his father are homeless and live in an airport. His father works as a janitor but doesn't make enough money for a home.

Oliver Button Is a Sissy by Tomie dePaola. Oliver Button does not like to do typical "boy" things, like play ball. He likes to walk in the woods, dress up, sing and dance, draw, and read books. Kids at school (and even his own father) call him a "sissy."

City Green by DyAnne DiSalvo-Ryan. A girl gets her neighborhood to join together to clean up an empty lot and plant a garden. This is a similar story to Paul Fleishman's wonderful short novel, *Seedfolks*.

The Middle Passage by Tom Feelings. The story of the Middle Passage, the ocean route used by ships bringing slaves to North America. The book has no text but gorgeous—yet graphically honest—drawings of slavery and life on the Middle Passage.

Weslandia by Paul Fleischman. Wesley is an original thinker who follows his passions and ideals and revels in marching to his own drummer, and he does not care that all of his friends and even his own parents think he's odd.

Kids at Work: Lewis Hine and the Crusade Against Child Labor by Russell Freedman. The story of Lewis Hine, the activist photographer whose pictures of child labor in the early twentieth century helped to end the injustice. The book includes many of Hine's photographs.

The Life and Death of Crazy Horse by Russell Freedman. The story of the great Oglala Sioux Chief, with wonderful pictures.

Teammates by Peter Golenbock. The story of the terrible racism endured by Jackie Robinson when he broke the race barrier in the major leagues, and the heroic support of his white teammate, Pee Wee Reese.

The Journey: Japanese Americans, Racism, and Renewal by Sheila Hamanaka. Based on Hamanaka's eight- by twenty-five-foot mural of the history of Japanese Americans. The story extends far beyond the oppression and labeling of Japanese Americans (the "Yellow Peril"), including references to World War II, Pearl Harbor, the Holocaust, the dropping of the atomic bombs on Hiroshima and Nagasaki, the Ku Klux Klan, McCarthyism and the "Red Scare," the Civil Rights Movement, and the anti–Vietnam war movement.

Hey, Little Ant by Phillip and Hannah Hoose. One of my favorite picture books. A boy has his foot raised and is about to stomp down on an ant. The ant pleads with the boy to not lower his foot. This is a great story to explore power and decision making, especially with younger kids.

A Band of Angels by Deborah Hopkinson. A fictionalized story of the real Jubilee Singers, a group of African American ex-slaves who formed a singing group and traveled the country and, eventually, Europe.

Waiting to Sing by Howard Kaplan. A family who loves music, is devastated when the mother dies, but music helps to bring them back together.

The Great Migration by Jacob Lawrence. A book based on the Great Migration series of paintings by the late African American artist Jacob Lawrence. The paintings tell the story of the migration of African Americans from slavery to Jim Crow to the migration from the South to the North.

From Slave Ship to Freedom Road by Julius Lester. The story of slavery from the capture of slaves in Africa to their enslavement and fight for freedom on the Underground Railroad. This book directly asks the reader to put themselves in the shoes of slaves and the oppressors.

Pearl Moscowitz's Last Stand by Arthur A. Levine. Grandma Pearl chains herself to a Gingko tree to save it from being cut down. A great book.

This Land is My Land by George Littlechild. Littlechild, an artist, is a Seminole. In his words and pictures he tells the story of the oppression of his people.

Erandi's Braids by Antonio Hernandez Madrigal. Erandi, a little girl in the village of Patzcuaro, Mexico, volunteers to sell her hair to the barber so her poor family can buy a new fishing net. Based on historical fact. In the 1940s and 1950s merchants drove around Patzcuaro to buy the beautiful hair of the Tarascan women who needed money.

Snowflake Bentley by Jacqueline Briggs Martin. For me this book is about passion, and being passionate is being good. For nearly fifty years, Wilson Bentley dedicated his life to taking pictures of snowflakes. Imagine that.

Hiroshima No Pika (The Flash of Hiroshima) by Toshi Maruki. August 6, 1945, 8:15 A.M. A book about the dropping of the atomic bomb on Hiroshima. The story is of a little girl, Mii, running from the destruction with her mother and badly injured father. Based on a true story told to the author.

Richard Wright and the Library Card by William Miller. A fictionalized story based on an actual comment the African American novelist, Richard Wright, made about getting his first library card. Because he could not get a library card, being African American, a white co-worker secretly lets Wright use his.

Baseball Saved Us by Ken Mochizuki. During their imprisonment at Japanese internment (or concentration) camps during World War II, Japanese American boys escaped their anguish by playing baseball. Once a boy is freed he confronts prejudice on a little league baseball field.

Tomas and the Library Lady by Pat Mora. With the help of a local librarian, the young son of Mexican American migrant farm workers falls in love with books and reading.

The Big Box by Toni Morrison. Patty, Mickey, and Lisa Sue are "feisty" kids who can't handle their freedom, so the adults in their lives (teachers, parents, and neighbors) keep them in a big box with everything they could possibly want.

The Paper Bag Princess by Robert Munsch. A well-known book for younger kids about a princess who rescues her prince in distress.

Wings by Christopher Myers. A boy, Ikarus, has wings and can fly. But his peers and the adults around him tease him and treat him as an outcast because he's "different." Myers also did the gorgeous illustrations.

Pink and Say by Patricia Polacco. A friendship between two boys, Pink and Say, one white and the other black, both fighting for the Union during the American Civil War. One of the most emotionally moving read-alouds a teacher can choose.

The Patchwork Quilt by Patricia Polacco. The story of a quilt as it passes through the generations of Polacco's family.

Aunt Chip and the Great Triple Creek Dam Affair by Patricia Polacco. Eli and his Aunt Chip live in Triple Creek. Once the big TV tower was built years ago people stopped reading books. All people do in Triple Creek (except Aunt Chip) is watch TV. Aunt Chip teaches Eli how to read, shows him the wonder of books, and eventually the great TV tower comes crashing down.

Why? by Nikolai Popov. This book has no words. The story of two frogs who have an innocent disagreement that escalates into complete war and destruction. A profound idea told in a way that even young kids can understand.

If a Bus Could Talk: The Story of Rosa Parks by Faith Ringgold. A telling of Rosa Parks' activism by refusing to give up her bus seat to a white man.

Whitewash by Ntozake Shange. A deeply powerful book about a racist incident on a little girl and the damage that it causes.

Starry Messenger by Peter Sis. The story of Galileo, whom the Catholic Church condemned during the Renaissance for his teaching and writing of astronomy. Galileo stands as a symbol of the repression of ideas and not allowing people to think for themselves and freely communicate.

Madlenka by Peter Sis. A little girl, Madlenka, has a loose tooth and wants to tell everyone! She runs around her block in New York City and tells all of her friends who run the local shops and businesses, all of whom have immigrated from another country. A gorgeously illustrated story about the goodness of a culturally diverse world.

When Gogo Went to Vote by Elinor Batezat Sisulu. The author lives in Capetown, South Africa, and her book tells the story of Thambi's great-grandmother, a black South African, who goes to vote for the first time in 1994.

Tikvah: Children's Book Creators Reflect on Human Rights. Published by SeaStar Books. *Tikvah* means "hope." More than forty children's book authors and illustrators have written short essays and created a wide variety of illustrations on different human rights issues from around the world.

Subway Sparrow by Leyla Torres. Four people from different cultures sit apart in a subway car. When a sparrow flies into the car, they work together to catch the bird and set it free.

Faithful Elephants by Yukio Truchiya. During World War II the Japanese government was concerned that if they were bombed, the wild animals in the Bonzai Zoo in Tokyo would roam free. They ordered all the zoo animals to be killed. A true story.

A Chair For My Mother by Vera B. Williams. Rosa, whose mother is a waitress, tells the story of her family saving coins to buy a new chair after all of their furniture is lost in a fire. The story has much goodness when the neighbors help Rosa's family after the fire.

The Other Side by Jacqueline Woodson. The homes of two girls, one African American and the other white, are separated by a fence. Slowly the two girls come together and hope for a day when the fence is torn down. A simple, yet beautiful story.

Encounter by Jane Yolen. The story of Christopher Columbus told from the perspective of the Taino Indians, whom the Spaniards completely killed off in less than one hundred years.

William's Doll by Charlotte Zolotow. Little William wants a doll, but his friends and his father think dolls are for girls. His grandma thinks differently.

Fifty Novels

My Name is Maria Isabel by Alma Flor Ada. Maria, a third grader at a new school, is saddened when her teacher won't call her by her real name. Her teachers says, "We already have two Marias in this class. Why don't we call you Mary instead?"

Nothing But the Truth by Avi. A seemingly small act of silliness and defiance by fifteen-year-old Brian sends things out of control in school.

Lupita Manana by Patricia Beatty. Thirteen-year-old Lupita and her brother Salvadore enter the United States illegally from Mexico to help their mother financially.

The Journal of Jesse Smoke by Joseph Bruchac. A fictional journal of a Cherokee boy, Jesse Smoke, as his tribe is forced onto the Trail of Tears.

Year of Impossible Goodbyes by Sook Nyul Choi. A fictionalized story of the author's harrowing escape from North Korea at the end of World War II. The story continues in Choi's *Echoes of the White Elephant.*

Dear Mr. Henshaw by Beverly Cleary. Leigh, a second grader and the new kid in school, is lonely and angry. His parents are divorced and his father is away driving trucks. Leigh writes to his favorite author and starts writing in a journal.

The Bumblebee Flies Anyway by Robert Cormier. One of my favorite young adult authors, Robert Cormier writes books that are powerfully honest and real. This book tells the story of Brian, a terminally ill boy who is admitted to an experimental hospital.

We All Fall Down by Robert Cormier. A complex story of random violence and its consequences. A deep, moral book for older readers.

The Chocolate War by Robert Cormier. The classic book about Robby, a private school student, who refuses to participate in his class' candy sale or his school's secret club.

Sadako and the Thousand Paper Cranes by Eleanor Coerr. Based on a true story of a girl, Sadako, in the hospital with radiation sickness ten years after the dropping of the atomic bomb on Hiroshima.

Killing Mr. Griffin by Lois Duncan. High school students kidnap their English teacher, with tragic results.

Seedfolks by Paul Fleischman. One of my favorite books, especially because it can be used with every grade from kindergarten through high school. One by one the residents of a Cleveland neighborhood help transform a polluted plot of land. The picture book *City Green* (see previous section) tells a similar story.

Whirligig by Paul Fleischman. After drinking at a party, fifteen-year-old Brett kills a high school girl by drunk driving. His compensation to the girl's family is to travel the United States to build four whirligigs in her honor, one in each corner of the country.

Flying Solo by Ralph Fletcher. What happens in a sixth-grade classroom when the substitute teacher doesn't show up and no one in the school realizes this?

The Lord of the Flies by William Golding. This is the only book on the children's literature list that was not written for children. It's one of my favorite novels and can be a catalyst for so many discussions and activities about being good. (It's a good read-aloud.) A planeload of ten-year-old boys crash-lands in the ocean. They're stranded on an uninhabited island with no adults and end up making war. A classic.

Witness by Karen Hesse. The Ku Klux Klan comes to a Vermont town in 1924. Fourteen characters switch off telling their perspectives.

Out of the Dust by Karen Hesse. Ten-year-old Billie Jo struggles to survive during the Depression in the dust bowl of Oklahoma. A deeply powerful book.

The Outsiders by S.E. Hinton. The classic story of boys confronting the complexities of life and gangs in the 1960s.

When Zachary Beaver Came to Town by Kimberly Willis Holt. Toby befriends Zachary Beaver, the "fattest boy in the world," when he visits town as part of a sideshow.

Sweetgrass by Jan Hudson. Sweetgrass, a fifteen-year-old Blackfoot Native Canadian girl, helps her family survive in the 1830s.

Spite Fever by Trudy Krisher. This is the story of thirteen-year-old Maggie, who is white, struggling to make sense of the racism and anger that surrounds her small town in Georgia in 1960. A powerful book for older kids.

Number the Stars by Lois Lowry. Three Jewish girls are hiding from the Nazis in Denmark during World War II.

The Giver by Lois Lowry. The world is now perfect, and twelve-year-old Jonas is given the prize job of being trained by The Giver, the official holder of memories. Soon, however, all is not nearly as perfect as it seems.

Baby by Patricia MacLachlan. A family living on an island on the Northeast coast find an abandoned baby with a note from the mother asking for her baby, Sophie, to be taken care of, and that one day she will return.

Parrot in the Oven by Victor Martinez. A beautifully written book about fourteen-year-old Manny Hernandez growing up in the barrio with an abusive and alcoholic father.

Junebug by Alice Mead. Fourth grader Reeve, or "Junebug," has big hopes of getting away from the housing projects where he lives with his sister and mother.

Monster by Walter Dean Myers. Steve, a high school student, is on trial for participating in a robbery/murder. Myers tells the story of his trial in a script format, as if it were a movie.

Scorpions by Walter Dean Myers. Jamal's brother is in jail for killing someone, and he wants Jamal, who is thirteen years old, to run his gang, the Scorpions.

Journey to Jo'Burg by Beverly Naidoo. Naledi and her brother Tiro live in South Africa. When their little sister becomes ill they set out on a long trek to get their mother, a maid for a white family. A short book.

No Turning Back by Beverly Naidoo. The story of Sipho, an impoverished boy on the run in South Africa just after the end of Apartheid.

Shiloh by Phyllis Reynolds Naylor. A boy steals a dog that is being abused by its owner.

The Great Gilly Hopkins by Katherine Paterson. Ten-year-old Gilly is kicked around from foster home to foster home, hoping one day to be reunited with her mother.

Lyddie by Katherine Paterson. Lyddie, a poor farm girl in the nineteenth century, must work in oppressive factories in Massachusetts.

Nightjohn by Gary Paulsen. Sarney, a twelve-year-old slave, tells her story. A short, honest, and at times graphic account of slavery. Paulsen wrote a sequel, *Sarney*.

The Day No Pigs Would Die by Robert Newton Peck. The story of Peck's childhood growing up poor during the Great Depression on a Quaker farm in Vermont. One of my favorites.

Freak the Mighty by Rodman Philbeck. "Freak" is a physically handicapped boy genius, and "the Mighty" is a huge kid who is seen as "dumb." Once they get together they become Freak the Mighty. A great book.

Walking to the Bus-Rider Blues by Harriette Gillem Robinet. Historical fiction of the 1956 Montgomery, Alabama, bus boycott during the Civil Rights Movement.

Esperanza Rising by Pam Munroz Ryan. Based on the life of Ryan's grandmother, this is the story of Esperanza, an affluent girl in Mexico who must flee with her mother and ends up as a migrant farm worker in the United States during the Great Depression.

Missing May by Cynthia Rylant. Twelve-year-old Summer has lived with her Aunt May and Uncle Ob for six years. Both Summer and Uncle Ob must confront their grief after Aunt May dies.

Holes by Louis Sachar. The adventures of Stanley Yelnats, who winds up in Camp Green Lake, a boys' detention center, digging a lot of holes.

Under the Blood-Red Sun by Graham Salisbury. Thirteen-year-old Tomikazu Nakaji and his Japanese American family are living in Hawaii when Pearl Harbor is attacked.

The Alfred Summer by Jan Slepian. Four outcasts, including one boy with cerebral palsy, come together to build a boat in a basement.

Maniac Magee by Jerry Spinelli. Jerry "Maniac" Magee is on the run after he leaves his aunt and uncle, helping to bring together two alienated sides of town.

Baseball in April by Gary Soto. A collection of short stories about everyday life for Latino boys growing up in northern California.

The Friendship by Mildred D. Taylor. This short book tells the story of four African American children who witness a racist confrontation in Mississippi in the 1930s.

Roll of Thunder, Hear My Cry by Mildred Taylor. The story of the African American Logan family, working together to survive the racism and fear of the Depression-era South. Two more books continue the story.

Journey Home by Yoshiko Uchida. Yuki and her Japanese American family are released from an internment camp during World War II and must work to put their lives back together. This continues the story begun in Uchida's first book, *Journey to Topaz*.

Making Up Megaboy by Virginia Walter and Katrina Roeckelein. For apparently no reason, a thirteen-year-old boy walks into a liquor store and shoots the owner. A very short book with a lot of mixed-media graphics.

Homeless Bird by Gloria Whelan. Koly, a thirteen-year-old girl in India, is married in an arranged marriage. She does not want to do this and must confront her own culture.

The Devil's Arithmetic by Jane Yolen. A Jewish girl, Hannah, is suddenly transported back to Nazi-occupied Poland.

Twenty-five Nonfiction Books

Herstory: Women Who Changed the World by Ruth Ashby and Deborah Gore Ohrn. A collection of biographies of 120 women throughout history. A fantastic resource of history that is rarely taught in school.

Parallel Journeys by Eleanor Ayer, with Helen Waterford and Alfons Heck. The true story of two boys growing up in Nazi Germany. One ends up in a concentration camp and the other ends up as a Nazi soldier. Much of the book is from interviews of the two as grown men.

33 Things Every Girl Should Know About Women's History: From Suffragettes to Skirt Length to the ERA by Tonya Bolden. A wonderful collection of writings on women's history. By the author of *33 Things Every Girl Should Know: Stories, Songs, Poems, and Smart Talk by 33 Extraordinary Women*.

China Son by Da Chen. Similar to Ji Li Jiang's memoir (see below), this is Chen's story of growing up during the Cultural Revolution in China.

We Shall Not Be Moved by Joan Dash. The powerful story of the women's factory strikes of 1909. This is a story of women's history that is typically ignored in school.

Bound for the North Star: True Stories of Fugitive Slaves by Dennis Brindell Fradin. The story slavery, the Underground Railroad, and abolitionists in the United States. An excellent resource.

Eleanor Roosevelt: A Life of Discovery by Russell Freedman. A biography of Eleanor Roosevelt, who as an outspoken activist was much more than merely a president's wife.

Red Scarf Girl by Ji Li Jiang. A memoir of growing up in China during Mao's Cultural Revolution.

Making Our Way: America at the Turn of the Century in the Words of the Poor and Powerless by William Loren Katz and Jacqueline Hunt Katz. A collection of primary source narratives giving voice to those so often silenced by society and schools.

Jefferson's Children: The Story of One American Family by Shannon Lanier and Jane Feldman. The story of Thomas Jefferson fathering two sets of descendants, first with his wife Martha, and second with his slave, Sally Hemmings. Much of the book is essays written by many of Jefferson's descendants—both white and African American.

Hopscotch Around the World by Mary D. Lankford. In a picture book format (with a lot of text) we learn how kids play hopscotch all around the world. This book combines playing with culture, both of which are being good.

To Be a Slave by Julius Lester. Oral histories of real slaves, from their capture in Africa to life on the plantations to emancipation.

Freedom's Children: Young Civil Rights Activists Tell Their Own Stories by Ellen Levine. A collection of oral histories of children who worked in the Civil Rights Movement. This is primary source material of children telling their own stories of oppression and activism.

No Pretty Pictures: A Child of War by Anita Lobel. The author's memoir of surviving the Holocaust.

Bread and Roses: The Struggle of American Labor, 1865–1915 by Milton Meltzer. The story of oppressive working conditions during the American Industrial Revolution and the growth of unions.

There Comes a Time: The Struggle for Civil Rights by Milton Meltzer. The story of the Civil Rights Movement—including information and pictures not commonly found in textbooks—by one of the best writers of nonfiction for children.

Voices from the Civil War by Milton Meltzer. A collection of primary sources from the American Civil War, such as letters, interviews, diaries, speeches, and newspaper articles.

Rosa Parks: My Story by Rosa Parks and Jim Haskins. An autobiography of the civil rights activist. Parks includes the time she spent at the Highlander Folk School in Tennessee where she learned about activism prior to her refusing to give up her seat on an Alabama bus.

Let It Shine by Andrea Davis Pinkney. A collection of stories of African American women who fought for freedom in a variety of ways. The short biographies include the less than well known activists, such as Biddy Mason and Fannie Lou Hamer, and the more well known, such as Harriet Tubman and Shirley Chisholm.

Stuff: The Secret Lives of Everyday Things by John C. Ryan and Alan Thein Durning. A short and unique book that shows the consequences of rampant consumerism by average Americans. The authors show the environmental costs of consuming everyday things, from coffee to gym shoes.

One Small Square: Pond by Donald M. Silver. One of the books in a large *One Small Square* series on nature. Each book takes one small square of a specific ecosystem (a swamp, the woods, a pond, etc.) and examines in detail the life teeming within it. These books can help students (especially younger kids) appreciate the wonders of the natural world and learn to treat it with respect.

Big Annie of Calumet: A True Story of the Industrial Revolution by Jerry Stanley. The story of Annie Clemenc, a labor activist during the 1913 copper miners' strike.

Leon's Story by Leon Walter Tillage. Leon Tillage's short memoir of growing up as an African American and confronting racism and intolerance. This is a short, easy to read, yet deeply powerful book.

The Invisible Thread by Yoshiko Uchida. The author tells the story of her family being forced into a Japanese American internment camp during World War II.

Focus: Five Women Photographers: Julia Margaret Cameron/Margaret Bourke-White/Flor Garuno/Sandy Skoglund/Lorna Simpson by Sylvia Wolf. Compares the work of five very different female artists who saw the world—and photographed it—in very different ways. Includes pictures of their work.

Fifty Books Adults Can Read to Think About Being Good

Slaves in the Family by Edward Ball

Rule of the Bone by Russell Banks

Plain and Simple by Sue Bender

Parting the Waters by Taylor Branch

Bury My Heart at Wounded Knee by Dee Brown

Kindred by Octavia Butler

The Moral Intelligence of Children by Robert Coles

Newjack by Ted Conover

Rosa Lee by Leon Dash

White Noise by Don Delillo

Pilgrim at Tinker Creek by Annie Dillard

Nickel and Dimed by Barbara Ehrenreich

Breaking the News by James Fallows

365 Days by Ronald J. Glasser

Faster by James Gleick

Humanity: A Moral History of the 20th Century by Jonathan Glover

We Wish to Inform You That Tomorrow We Will Be Killed with Our Families by Philip Gourevitch

Lord of the Flies by William Golding

Who Will Tell the People: The Betrayal of American Democracy by William Grieder

The Autobiography of Malcom X by Alex Haley and Malcolm X

Dispatches by Michael Herr

Hiroshima by John Hersey

Our America: Life and Death on the South Side of Chicago by LeAlan Jones and Lloyd Newman, with David Isay

Savages by Joe Kane

The Poisonwood Bible by Barbara Kingsolver

No Logo by Naomi Klein

There Are No Children Here by Alex Kotlowitz

To Kill a Mockingbird by Harper Lee

Survival in Auschwitz by Primo Levi

The Color of Water by James McBride

The End of Nature by Bill McKibben

Material World by Peter Menzel

The Things They Carried by Tim O'Brien

Upside Down by Eduardo Orleando

Zen and the Art of Motorcycle Maintenance by Robert Pirsig

Dead Man Walking by Sister Helen Prejean

The Song of the Dodo by David Quamenn

Always Running by Luis Rodriguez

Push by Sapphire

Fast Food Nation by Eric Schlosser

The Overspent American by Juliet B. Schor

Homestead by William Serrin

Maus I and *Maus II* by Art Speigelman

Walden by Henry David Thoreau

The March of Folly by Barbara Tuchman

Night by Elie Wiesel

Leaves of Grass by Walt Whitman

Native Son by Richard Wright

The Moral Animal by Robert Wright

A People's History of the United States, 1492–Present by Howard Zinn

Twenty-five Books on Education
That Can Help Teachers Think About Being Good

Ideology and Curriculum by Michael Apple

Teacher by Sylvia Ashton-Warner

In the Middle by Nancie Atwell

Reading, Writing, and Rising Up: Teaching About Social Justice and the Power of the Written Word by Linda Christensen

Experience and Education by John Dewey

Making Justice Our Project edited by Carol Edelsky

Pedagogy of the Oppressed by Paulo Freire

The Dialectic of Freedom by Maxine Greene

Releasing the Imagination: Essays on Education, the Arts, and Social Change by Maxine Greene

How Children Fail by John Holt

Teaching to Transgress by bell hooks

On the Brink: Negotiating Literature and Life with Adolescents by Susan Hynds

Punished by Rewards by Alfie Kohn

Savage Inequalities by Jonathan Kozol

Lies My Teacher Told Me by James Loewen

Contradictions of Control: School Structure and School Knowledge by Linda M. McNeil

The Power of Their Ideas by Deborah Meier

Holler If You Hear Me by Gregory Michie

The Universal Schoolhouse by James Moffett

The Light in Their Eyes: Creating Multicultural Learning Communities by Sonia Nieto

The Challenge to Care in Schools: An Alternative Approach to Education by Nel Noddings

You Can't Say You Can't Play by Vivian Gussin Paley

The Courage to Teach by Parker Palmer

Freedom to Learn by Carl Rogers

Lives on the Boundary by Mike Rose

References

Adler, S. 2000. "Creating Public Spaces in the Social Studies Classroom." *Social Education* 65(1): 6–7, 68–71.

Allen, J., et al. 2002 "PhOLKS lore: Learning from Photographs, Families, and Children." *Language Arts* 79(4): 312–322.

Atwell, N. 1998. *In the Middle: New Understandings About Writing, Reading, and Learning,* 2nd ed. Portsmouth, NH: Heinemann.

Ayers, W. 1995. *To Teach: The Journey of a Teacher.* New York: Teachers College Press.

Barber, B. 1985. *Strong Democracy: Participatory Democracy for a New Age.* Berkeley: University of California.

Berman, S. 1997. *Children's Social Consciousness and the Development of Social Responsibility.* Albany, NY: SUNY Press.

Bigelow, B. 2001. "Teaching About Unsung Heroes." In *Rethinking Our Classrooms: Teaching for Equity and Justice,* Volume 2, eds. B. Bigelow, B. Harvey, S. Karp, and L. Miller, 37–41. Milwaukee: Rethinking Schools.

Bomer, R. 1999. "Writing to Think Critically: The Seeds of Social Action." *Voices From the Middle* 6(4): 2–8.

Brazelton, T.B. 1992. *Touchpoints.* Reading, MA: Addison-Wesley.

Brodhagen, 1995. "The Situation Made Us Special." In *Democratic Schools,* eds. M. Apple and J.A. Beane. Alexandria, VA: Association for Supervision and Curriculum Development.

Brown, D. 2002. *Becoming a Successful Urban Teacher.* Portsmouth, NH: Heinemann.

Caine, R.N. and G. Caine, 1991. *Making Connections: Teaching and the Human Brain.* Alexandria, VA: Association for Supervision and Curriculum Development.

Calkins, Lucy McCormick. 2000. *The Art of Teaching Reading.* New York: Longman.

Chandler, T. 1998. "Use of Reframing as a Classroom Strategy." *Education* 119(2): 365–367.

Christensen, L. 2000. *Reading, Writing, and Rising Up: Teaching About Social Justice and the Power of the Written Word.* Milwaukee: Rethinking Schools.

Coles, R. 1997. *The Moral Intelligence of Children.* New York: Plume.

Csikszentmihalyi, M., K. Rathunde, and S. Whalen. 1994. *Talented Teenagers: The Roots of Success & Failure.* New York: Cambridge.

Delpit, L. 1988. "The Silenced Dialogue: The Power and Pedagogy in Educating Other People's Children." *Harvard Educational Review* 58(3): 280–298.

DeMarrias, K.B. and M.D. LeCompte. 1999. *The Way Schools Work: A Sociological Analysis of Education.* New York: Longman.

Dewey, J. 1944/1966. *Democracy and Education.* New York: The Free Press.

Eckholm, E. 2001. "China Said to Punish Unionist." *New York Times,* 9 February, A8, national edition.

Elbow, P. 1973. *Writing Without Teachers.* London: Oxford.

Engle, S. and S. Ochoa. 1988. *Education for Democratic Citizenship: Decision Making in the Social Studies*. New York: Teachers College Press.

Fenstermacher, G. 1990. "Some Moral Considerations on Teaching as a Profession." In *The Moral Dimensions of Teaching*, eds. J.I. Goodlad, R. Soder, and K. Sirotnik, 130–151. San Francisco: Jossey-Bass.

Fleming, D. 1996. "Preamble to a More Perfect Classroom." *Educational Leadership* 54: 73–76.

Foshay, A. 1997. "The Emotions and Social Studies." *Journal of Curriculum and Supervision* 12(4): 356–366.

Frazier, I. 2000. *On the Rez*. New York: Picador.

Gardner, H. 1983. *Frames of Mind: The Theory of Multiple Intelligences*. New York: Basic Books.

Gaughan, J. 1999. "From Literature to Language: Personal Writing and Critical Pedagogy." *English Education* 31(4): 310–326.

Glasser, W. 1969. *Schools Without Failure*. New York: Harper and Row.

Glover, J. 1999. *Humanity: A Moral History of the Twentieth Century*. New Haven, CT: Yale University Press.

Gorrell, N. 2000. "Teaching Empathy Through Ecphrastic Poetry: Entering a Curriculum of Peace." *English Journal* 89(5): 32–41.

Greene, M. 1988. *The Dialectic of Freedom*. New York: Teachers College Press.

Haberman, M. 1995. *Star Teachers of Children in Poverty*. West Lafayette, IN: Kappa Delta Pi.

Hansen, D.T. 1992. "The Emergence of a Shared Morality in a Classroom." *Curriculum Inquiry* 22(3): 345–361.

Hersey, J. 1956. *Hiroshima*. New York: Bantam.

Hynds, S. 1997. *On the Brink: Negotiating Literature and Life with Adolescents*. New York: Teachers College Press.

Kilpatrick, W.H. 1918. "The Project Method." *Teachers College Press* 19(4): 319–355.

Kliebard, H.M. 1987. *The Struggle for the American Curriculum 1893–1958*. New York: Routledge.

Klinkenborg, V. 2000. "The Conscience of Place: Sand Creek." *Mother Jones*, November/December.

Kohn, A. 1993. *Punished by Rewards: The Trouble with Gold Stars, Incentive Plans, A's, Praise, and Other Bribes*. Boston: Houghton Mifflin.

Kohn, A. 1996. *Beyond Discipline: From Compliance to Community*. Alexandria, VA: Association for Supervision and Curriculum Development.

Kornfield, J. and J. Goodman. 1995. "Melting the Glaze: Exploring Student Responses to Liberatory Social Studies." *Theory Into Practice* 37(4): 306–313.

Kretovics, J. 1985. "Critical Literacy: Challenging the Assumptions of Mainstream Educational Theory." *Journal of Education* 167(2): 50–62.

Ladson-Billings, G. 1994. *The DreamKeepers: Successful Teachers of African American Children*. San Francisco: Jossey-Bass.

Lee, E. 1995. "Interview with Enid Lee: Taking Multicultural Anti-Racist Education Seriously." In *Rethinking Schools: An Agenda for Change*, eds. D. Levine, et al. New York: The New Press.

Levine, E. 1993. *Freedom's Children: Young Civil Rights Activists Tell Their Own Stories*. New York: Puffin.

Loewen, J. 1994. *Lies My Teacher Told Me*. New York: Touchstone.

Mayher, J. 1990. *Uncommon Sense: Theoretical Practice in Language Education*. Portsmouth, NH: Heinemann.

McGregor, D. 1960. *The Human Side of Enterprise*. New York: McGraw-Hill.

McNeil, D.G. 2001. "Cosmetic Saves a Cure for Sleeping Sickness." *New York Times*, 9 February, A1, A8, national edition.

McNeil, L. 1988. *Contradictions of Control: School Structure and School Knowledge*. New York: Routledge.

Menzel, P. 1995. *Material World*. San Francisco: Sierra Club Books.

Noddings, N. 1992. *The Challenge to Care in Schools: An Alternative Approach to Education*. New York: Teachers College Press.

Orr, D. 1995. "Educating for the Environment." *Change* 27(3): 43–46.

Paley, V.G. 1992. *You Can't Say You Can't Play*. Cambridge, MA: Harvard.

Peterson, B. 1994. "Teaching for Social Justice: One Teacher's Journey." In *Rethinking Our Classrooms: Teaching for Equity and Social Justice*, eds. B. Bigelow, L. Christensen, S. Karp, B. Miner, and B. Peterson, 30–38. Milwaukee: Rethinking Schools.

Peterson, B. 2001a. "Teaching Math Across the Curriculum: A Fifth-Grade Teacher Battles 'Number Numbness.'" In *Rethinking Our Classrooms: Teaching for Equity and Social Justice*, Volume 2, eds. B. Bigelow, B. Harvey, S. Karp, and L. Miller, 84–88. Milwaukee: Rethinking Schools.

Peterson, B. 2001b. Rethinking the U.S. Constitutional Convention: A Role Play. In *Rethinking Our Classrooms: Teaching for Equity and Social Justice*, Volume 2, eds. B. Bigelow, B. Harvey, S. Karp, and L. Miller, 84–88. Milwaukee: Rethinking Schools.

Preskill, S. 1997. "Discussion, Schooling, and the Struggle for Democracy." *Theory and Research in Social Education* 25(3): 316-345.

Proctor, V. and K. Kantor. 1996. "Social Justice Notebooks." *Voices from the Middle* 3(2): 31–35.

Purpel, D. 1999. *Moral Outrage in Education*. New York: Peter Lang.

Reif, L. 1992. *Seeking Diversity: Language Arts with Adolescents*. Portsmouth, NH: Heinemann.

Rogers, C. 1969. *Freedom to Learn*. Columbus, OH: Charles E. Merrill.

Sanneh, K. 2001. "Hearing the Voices of Hip-Hop." *New York Times*, 9 February, A27, national edition.

Schrank, J. 1972. *Teaching Human Beings: 101 Subversive Activities for the Classroom*. Boston: Beacon Press.

Shannon, P. 1995. *Text, Lies, and Videotape*. Portsmouth, NH: Heinemann.

Singer, P. 1999. "The Singer Solution to World Poverty." *New York Times Magazine*, 5 September.

Smith, F. 1986. *Insult to Intelligence: The Bureaucratic Invasion into Our Classrooms*. Portsmouth, NH: Heinemann.

Whelan, G. 2000. *Homeless Bird*. New York: Harper Trophy.

Wolk, S. 1994. "Adolescents, Poetry, and Trust." *Language Arts* 71(2): 108–114.

Wolk, S. 1998. *A Democratic Classroom*. Portsmouth, NH: Heinemann.

Zeichner, K. and D. Liston. (1987). *Reflective Teaching*. Mahwah, NJ: Lawrence Erlbaum Associates.

Wolk, S. 2001. "The Benefits of Exploratory Time." *Educational Leadership* 59(2): 56–59.

Index